HOW TO INTERPRET
THE CONSTITUTION

How to Interpret the Constitution

CASS R. SUNSTEIN

PRINCETON UNIVERSITY PRESS

PRINCETON & OXFORD

Requests for permission to reproduce material from this work should be sent to permissions@press.princeton.edu

Published by Princeton University Press
41 William Street, Princeton, New Jersey 08540
99 Banbury Road, Oxford OX2 6JX

press.princeton.edu

All Rights Reserved

Library of Congress Control Number: 2023900432

ISBN 9780691252049
ISBN (e-book) 9780691252056

British Library Cataloging-in-Publication Data is available

Editiorial: Bridget Flannery-McCoy, Alena Chekanov
Jacket: Chris Ferrante
Production: Erin Suydam
Publicity: James Schneider, Kate Farquhar-Thomson

This book has been composed in Arno Pro

Printed on acid-free paper. ∞

Printed in the United States of America

10 9 8 7 6 5 4 3 2 1

What then is the wisdom of the times called old? Is it the wisdom of gray hairs? No.—It is the wisdom of the cradle.

—JEREMY BENTHAM

The most violent revolutions in an individual's beliefs leave most of his old order standing. Time and space, cause and effect, nature and history, and one's own biography remain untouched. New truth is always a go-between, a smoother-over of transitions. It marries old opinion to new fact so as ever to show a minimum of jolt, a maximum of continuity.

—WILLIAM JAMES

TABLE OF CONTENTS

HOW TO INTERPRET
THE CONSTITUTION

Introduction

IN FEBRUARY 2021, I started a new job as Senior Counselor in the U.S. Department of Homeland Security. Before I began, I was required, or privileged, to take the oath of office. The United States was in the midst of the COVID-19 pandemic, and so I took the oath all by myself, online via my 2015 MacBook Air, in a little room in my home.

Here is what I was asked to say:

> I do solemnly swear that I will support and defend the Constitution of the United States against all enemies, foreign and domestic; that I will bear true faith and allegiance to the same; that I take this obligation freely, without any mental reservation or purpose of evasion; and that I will well and faithfully discharge the duties of the office on which I am about to enter: So help me God.

Before I started, I thought to myself: This is a great honor, and it is just my laptop and me, and the single person administering the oath; *I will not cry.*

Reader, I cried.

Here's one reason. The house in which I took the oath is in Concord, Massachusetts. That house was built in 1763 by

Ephraim Wood, an active participant in the activities that led to the American Revolution. As I took the oath, I looked out on my front yard, where British soldiers came on April 19, 1775— the first day of the American Revolution.[1]

Four years earlier, Wood had been chosen as chairman of Concord's selectmen, town clerk, and assessor and overseer of the poor. (Later he was reelected to those offices—seventeen times.) In 1773 he served on the committee that decided to protest the tax on tea. According to the Massachusetts Historical Commission, the Wood House, as it is called, is "one of the most important of Concord's early farmhouses."[2] The house played a significant role in the Revolutionary War. Actually, it helped precipitate the fighting. It was one of the places where munitions were being held, which is what prompted the initial British invasion.

"In the weeks before April 19, 1775," explains the Historical Commission, "when military stores were being sent inland to Concord for hiding, six of 35 barrels of powder and some bullets were hidden on Ephraim Wood's farm." Hours before shots were fired, the British forces went to that farm, looking for the munitions and also for Wood. They didn't find him. Their plans were less secret than they thought, and Wood managed to escape, carrying munitions on his back.

On that critical day, British soldiers destroyed a lot of property, including every public store that they could find. But they didn't burn down or even damage Wood's house. Wood returned. As the fighting continued, became terrible, and then worse, the house remained intact. It was there before the

---

1. For a fuller description of the house and its history, on which I draw here, see Cass R. Sunstein, *Impeachment: A Citizen's Guide* (2017).

2. Quoted in Betsy Levinson, "Home Portrait: Country Charm Meets Modern Amenities," *Wicked Local Concord*, October 5, 2015.

colonies turned into the United States, and it was there when Jefferson wrote the Declaration of Independence. Just a few months after Jefferson did that, Wood himself, a short distance from his house, helped write a document that called for a Constitutional Convention in Concord,[3] resolving:

> That the supreme Legislative, Either in their proper capacity or in Joint Committee are by no means a Body Proper to form & Establish a Constitution of form of Government for Reasones following viz—first Because we conceive that Constitution, in its proper idea intends a system of principals established to secure the subject in the Possession of, and enjoyment of their Rights & Privileges against any encroachment of the Governing Part.

Wood's group has been credited with inventing the whole idea of a convention for constitution-making. His house was there when the Articles of Confederation ruled the land, and it was there when the Federalist Papers were written and when the Constitution was ratified. It stands proudly today.

When I took the oath on my little laptop, there in the house that Ephraim Wood built back in 1763 and that survived the British invasion in 1775 and helped precipitate the Revolutionary War, I was keenly aware of all this (and so I might be forgiven for crying).

What did I take the oath to "support and defend"? In 1789, nearly two years after the Constitution had been written, James Jackson, a representative from Georgia, observed, "Our Constitution is like a vessel just launched, and lying at the wharf,

---

3. See Roger Sherman Hoar, "When Concord Invented the Constitutional Convention" (July 3, 1917), available at http://constitutionathomeandabroad.blogspot.com/2012/05/when-concord-invented-constitutional.html?m=1.

she is untried, and you can hardly discover any one of her properties."[4] That is one conception of the founding document, at least in the late eighteenth century, and perhaps even to some extent today. Far from being a system of specific rules and concrete commands, the Constitution can be seen as a vessel whose properties have been discovered (or created?) over a period of centuries. Those properties are still being discovered (and created).

Here are a few excerpts from the Constitution. Pause over the words, if you would, and try to read them as if they were new.

> All legislative Powers herein granted shall be vested in a Congress of the United States, which shall consist of a Senate and House of Representatives.

> The Congress shall have Power to lay and collect Taxes, Duties, Imposts and Excises, to pay the Debts and provide for the common Defence and general Welfare of the United States; but all Duties, Imposts and Excises shall be uniform throughout the United States;

> No Bill of Attainder or ex post facto Law shall be passed.

> The executive Power shall be vested in a President of the United States of America.

> The President, Vice President and all civil Officers of the United States, shall be removed from Office on Impeachment for, and Conviction of, Treason, Bribery, or other high Crimes and Misdemeanors.

> Congress shall make no law respecting an establishment of religion, or prohibiting the free exercise thereof; or abridging the freedom of speech, or of the press.

---

4. See Jonathan Gienapp, *The Second Creation* (2018), 1.

A well regulated Militia, being necessary to the security of a free State, the right of the people to keep and bear Arms, shall not be infringed.

The enumeration in the Constitution, of certain rights, shall not be construed to deny or disparage others retained by the people.

All persons born or naturalized in the United States, and subject to the jurisdiction thereof, are citizens of the United States and of the State wherein they reside. No State shall make or enforce any law which shall abridge the privileges or immunities of citizens of the United States; nor shall any State deprive any person of life, liberty, or property, without due process of law; nor deny to any person within its jurisdiction the equal protection of the laws.

What do these words mean? How shall we interpret them? Are they fixed and firm? Does their scope change over time? What room, if any, does the current generation—judges, politicians, all of us—have to give them meaning?

"Congress shall make no law . . . abridging the freedom of speech." Do those words forbid Congress from punishing speakers if they incite people to commit federal crimes?

"No State shall make or enforce any law which shall abridge the privileges or immunities of citizens of the United States." Does that mean that states must recognize same-sex marriages?

"A well regulated Militia, being necessary to the security of a free State, the right of the people to keep and bear Arms, shall not be infringed." Does that prohibit the government from requiring people to get a license to carry guns in public?

How do we go about answering such questions? What is our theory of interpretation? Do we have to have one?

The United States is in a period of constitutional upheaval, in which long-standing understandings are being jettisoned and new ones are taking their place. Before our eyes, something like a new Constitution is being born.

Some conservatives once spoke nostalgically and with firm resolve about "the Constitution in Exile." That was the Constitution as it existed in the early 1930s, before Franklin Delano Roosevelt's New Deal, the rise of the modern administrative state, and the emergence of a right to privacy, including the right to use contraceptives. In the early 1930s our institutions and our rights were dramatically different from what they are now. No Social Security Administration, no National Labor Relations Board, no Environmental Protection Agency—and no sex equality, let alone a right to same-sex marriage. The old Constitution, the critics claimed, was the real Constitution, and it was lost.

That old Constitution is coming out of exile. What we are seeing is, in important respects, in the nature of a regime change, or a paradigm shift. Any snapshot will rapidly go out of date, but consider the following:

- The right to choose abortion has been eliminated;
- The right to privacy, as such, is in deep trouble;
- The individual right to possess guns, first recognized in 2008, is being expanded;
- The rights of religious believers are rapidly growing;
- Affirmative action is on its heels, and it might well be eliminated;
- Commercial advertising is being protected more than ever before;
- Expenditures on political campaigns are being treated like political speech;

- People's rights to sue the government are being radically curtailed;
- Property rights are expanding; and
- The administrative state, and its efforts with respect to safety, health, and the environment, are under severe constitutional pressure (in some ways, this may be the most important development of all).

Twenty years from now, our rights and our institutions are bound to be very different from what they are today. They are already very different from what they were ten years ago.

One thing should be clear: There is an uncomfortable overlap between the views of the majority of the Supreme Court of the United States and the views of the right wing of the contemporary Republican Party. For those "originalists" who insist that the Court is simply "adhering to the written Constitution," that is a red flag. It would be a stunning coincidence if the Constitution as understood in (say) 1792 or 1871 turned out to match the convictions of a political party in 2022.

At the same time, it is crucial to see that the Court has been claiming to follow "the original public meaning" of the founding document and to discipline constitutional law by close reference to it. When the Court recognized an individual right to possess guns, it spoke of the original public meaning of the Second Amendment. In a similar vein, the Court has also been emphasizing the importance of long-standing traditions and suggesting that if those traditions do not recognize a right, it is no right at all. When the Court overruled *Roe v. Wade*, which had protected the right to abortion, it spoke of traditions. With these ideas in mind, the Court seems to be rebuilding constitutional law, almost from the ground up.

Two Goals

In this book I aim to step back from the current debates and explore more enduring questions. I have two main goals. First, I seek to provide a kind of primer, or a guide for the perplexed—an account of what diverse people are saying and doing about the Constitution of the United States, and why they are saying and doing it. My hope is that the account will clarify the nature of legitimate disagreement, whatever one ultimately concludes.

Why do "conservative" judges disagree with "progressive" judges? Why are some judges "originalists," and why do other judges abhor "originalism"? What are the various options? How shall we evaluate them? If we are not originalists, what might be we? My answers to these questions are meant to provide a conceptual map, one that shows why reasonable people offer different answers (and that also might show why some people are unreasonable). The conceptual map is intended to be highly sympathetic to diverse views, including those that I reject. We take as our guide here John Stuart Mill, who said, "He who knows only his own side of the case knows little of that."

Second, I seek to ask and answer a single question: *How should we choose a theory of constitutional interpretation?*

My answer is simple: Judges (and others) should choose the theory that would make the American constitutional order better rather than worse. That answer is meant to emphasize that when people disagree about constitutional interpretation, they are actually disagreeing about what would make the American constitutional order better rather than worse.

That claim is much less innocuous than it might seem. It has bite. It rejects a widespread view, which is that a theory of constitutional interpretation might be "read off" the Constitution itself, or come from some abstract idea like "legitimacy" or

from the very idea of interpretation. For example, many "originalists" believe that their preferred approach is not a product of
a choice; they insist that the Constitution makes that choice.
The problem is that *the Constitution does not contain the instructions for its own interpretation.*

You might want to ask: Who decides what would make the
American constitutional order better rather than worse? If
you ask that question, you might mean to offer an objection
to my argument. Please stand down. The answer is: Anyone
trying to choose a theory of interpretation. Judges; legislators;
presidents; you; me; us. That's all there is. There's no one else.

It follows that any approach to constitutional interpretation
needs to be defended in terms of its effects, broadly conceived—
of what it does for our rights and our institutions. You might be
inclined to think that judges should be "originalists," or should
respect "democracy," or should not be "activists." You might
think that the rule of law and stability over time are of central
importance. You might think that the Supreme Court should
adopt a strong presumption in favor of the constitutionality of
what Congress and the president do—which means that the
Court should uphold most of such actions against constitutional attack. Or you might reject that idea and think that the
Supreme Court should take a strong stand in favor of certain
rights—say, the right to free speech or the right to religious
liberty. If so, the approach to interpretation that you favor must
be justified on the ground that it would make our constitutional
order better rather than worse (in terms of your own considered judgment about what counts as better and what counts as
worse), and it must be compared to alternatives.[5]

5. True, we have to be careful here. For judges, at least, a theory of interpretation
cannot be made up out of whole cloth. Suppose that a judge embraces a theory of

Reflective Equilibrium and Fixed Points

To cut to the chase: To defend a theory of interpretation, judges (and others) must seek a kind of "reflective equilibrium." The term comes from moral and political philosophy, where the search for reflective equilibrium plays a central role. In chapter 4, I will have a fair bit to say about what reflective equilibrium involves. For now, the basic idea is that we try to ensure that our moral and political judgments line up with one another, do not contradict each other, and support one another. We achieve reflective equilibrium when that happens. That idea might seem unfamiliar and mysterious, but the search for reflective equilibrium is actually common; in thinking through hard questions, and maybe even easy ones, you probably seek reflective equilibrium.

---

interpretation that is wildly out of step with two hundred years of American law, or even fifty such years. If so, she will have a lot of explaining to do, and it is not clear that any imaginable explanation will be sufficient. We need to distinguish between the theory of interpretation that an external observer might favor, were she permitted to adopt one on her own, and the theory of interpretation that a real-world judge might favor, given the fact that the judge is a real-world judge and a participant in a particular tradition. I will be assuming here that the reasonable candidates for a theory that an external observer might favor are already present, to a greater or lesser extent, within the American legal tradition. I do not merely assume that; I believe it to be true.

Of course I might be wrong on that point. There might be something new under the sun, and someone might find it or name it. You never know. But as we will soon see, the American legal tradition contains many candidates for a theory of interpretation. (You can decide which of them is reasonable.) I will be paying considerable attention to the question whether one or more of them would be inconsistent with large segments of American law. If they are, that is a problem. It may or may not be a decisive problem. But for both external observers and real-world judges, there is no escape from the question whether an approach would make the American legal system better rather than worse.

Suppose, for example, that you are trying to figure out what morality requires. How will you do that? If you are seeking reflective equilibrium, you will focus both on individual practices that seem to you to be self-evidently wrong and on theories that might explain why they are wrong. You want to bring order to your judgments; you test them against each other. For instance, you might be strongly inclined to believe that torture is wrong. That belief might be a provisional "fixed point" for you, in the sense that you will be deeply committed to it and exceptionally reluctant to give it up. In fact you might have a host of "fixed points," understood as judgments to which you are deeply committed. You might think that murder and rape are wrong, that lying is wrong, that assault is wrong, that theft is wrong. It might be that, for you, some of these thoughts are more fixed and firm than others. The most fixed convictions will play the largest role in your thinking. If a proposed theory suggests that slavery is permissible, you would be unlikely to find that theory acceptable.

I will be suggesting that the search for reflective equilibrium does, and must, play a central role in constitutional law. In fact, it is the only game in town. In deciding how to interpret the Constitution, we cannot pull a theory out of the sky, insist that it must be right, and declare victory. It is hopeless to try to justify a theory of interpretation by pointing to some large-sounding word, such as "legitimacy" or "democracy" or even "interpretation" (even though those words are relevant). Instead people must work to align their provisional judgments, described at multiple levels of generality. People might think that no theory of interpretation should allow unelected judges to do whatever they want; that is a provisional fixed point (and a good one). People might think that any theory of constitutional interpretation had better give a lot of protection to freedom of speech; for them, that is a provisional fixed point (and another good one). They might think that any theory of constitutional interpretation had better forbid torture; that is also a provisional fixed point (good once more). They might think that any theory of constitutional interpretation had better promote the rule of law, understood to include stable rules that are understandable and clear, and that apply to all, not just to some; that is also a provisional fixed point (very good indeed).

Some fixed points are not so provisional; people would be most unwilling to give them up. Oliver Wendell Holmes Jr. referred to his "Can't Helps," understood as his firmest convictions, the beliefs that he could not help but hold.[6] When I was clerking for Justice Thurgood Marshall in 1980, I once urged my boss to vote to strike down a government practice that I saw as horrific and fundamentally unfair. After we quarreled for about an hour, Marshall looked at me skeptically and exclaimed, "Okay, I'll use Felix's test. It don't make me puke!" It was decades later (in 2022) that I learned that Justice Felix Frankfurter did indeed say, in conference with his fellow justices, that a practice was not so offensive as to make him "puke."[7]

With all due deference to Marshall and Frankfurter, this is not the most lovely way to describe matters. We might say instead that people have some exceptionally strong convictions about what the Constitution must mean, forbid, or require, and that it would take a great deal to dislodge those convictions. It follows that people must explore how their firm judgments about particular cases (racial segregation, compulsory sterilization, sex discrimination, gun control) fare under potential

6. See Oliver Wendell Holmes Jr., Natural Law, *Har. L. Rev.* 32 (1918): 40.
7. See Brad Snyder, *Democratic Justice* (2022), 488.

theories of interpretation. If a theory would override those judgments, then that theory should be questioned. We need to go back and forth between possible theories and the outcomes that they produce. Theories might have a great deal of appeal in the abstract, but if they license the Supreme Court to strike down the Social Security Act, they might not be so appealing.

It is important to say that fixed points about constitutional law are not, or are not simply, fixed points about morality and justice. They have to be fixed points about constitutional law— as in the view that the First Amendment protects political dissent or the Eighth Amendment forbids torture. Those are not merely abstract claims about morality and justice. It is also important to reiterate that our fixed points operate at multiple levels of generality. They are not only about specific cases. We might have a commitment to federalism (however we understand it), which is abstract. We might have a commitment to self-government, which is also abstract, and a commitment to freedom of religion, which seems a bit less abstract, and a commitment to the idea that the government can impose taxes on everyone, which seems less abstract still. We might have a commitment to the idea that the Constitution does not allow governments to mandate school prayer, which is pretty particular.

Of course, it is true that our fixed points might turn out, on reflection, not to be so fixed. Some of our fixed points might ultimately be moral fixed points, not constitutional fixed points, and (one more time) the two are not the same. You might think, for example, that in a just society no one will starve, without also thinking that there is a constitutional right not to starve. And whether we are speaking of morality or constitutional law, what is fixed today might not be fixed a month, a year, or a decade from now. Constitutional law itself reflects that point. It

fixes and unfixes things. In 1930 it would have been pretty radical, and maybe even preposterous, to say that the Constitution
forbids racially segregated schools. As of this writing, it would
be radical, and quite preposterous, to say that the Constitution
does not forbid racially segregated schools. In 1980 it would
have been pretty radical, and maybe even preposterous, to say
that the Constitution requires states to recognize same-sex marriage. Just four decades later, it would have been a bit radical, if
not preposterous, to say that the Constitution does not require
states to recognize same-sex marriage. In 1990 it would have
been pretty radical, if not preposterous, to say that the Constitution creates an individual right to possess guns. As of this
writing, that right is entrenched in constitutional understandings. We can be confident that some of our fixed points about
constitutional law, right now (your fixed points, my fixed
points), will get unfixed in the next ten or twenty years, and we
(you and I) will wonder: How could we have thought that, way
back when?

All this is true and important. Humility and openness are
critical. Still: To know what theory to adopt, judges and others
must see if they can be satisfied that a proposed theory fits well,
or well enough, with their most deeply held views about particular cases—and also that the theory also fits well, or well
enough, with broad values involving the rule of law, self-
government, liberty, and equality.

I will have a lot more to say about the search for reflective
equilibrium; these should be taken as preliminary remarks.
That search, I will suggest, gives more specific answers to the
question of what judges (and others) are really disagreeing
about. Some judges would be dismayed to learn that their theory would mean that the Clean Air Act is unconstitutional;
others would be cheered. Some judges would be dismayed to

learn that a theory of interpretation would lead to a right to same-sex marriage; others would be delighted. Some judges would be dismayed to learn that their theory would grant judges considerable discretion to give content to the idea of "liberty"; others would be pleased. Some judges are appalled by the idea of judicial discretion; others are disturbed by it; still others welcome it. Their dismay, delight, or cheer matter, and should matter, to their views about what theory to adopt.

That is a central reason that judges (and others) disagree about how to interpret the Constitution. There is no God's-eye view here (or at least we do not have ready access to it).

One of my central claims is that "fixed points"—including convictions about what is good or right in particular cases—must play a central role in choices about the right theory of constitutional interpretation, and that to a remarkable degree they actually do so. If a theory would lead to the conclusion that racial segregation is constitutional, almost everyone in the modern era would question it. It should come as no surprise that exponents of various theories are at pains to explain why their preferred approach does not lead to that conclusion. Indeed, are typically at pains to show that their preferred approach leads to (many) wonderful results, and that if some bad results do follow from their preferred approach, they are not too many, and they are not too bad—or that if they seem bad, they are not bad at all (perhaps because democracy is what matters or will ride to the rescue).

I aim, then, to defend the proposition that any approach to constitutional interpretation must be justified on the ground that it would make our constitutional order better rather than worse. But I will also use that proposition to question some prominent theories of interpretation—including, and above all, originalism. The issues here are not straightforward, in part because originalism comes in many shapes and sizes, and it is not entirely clear what it entails. But the basic idea is that originalism would not have good consequences; it would lead to a system of constitutional law that is far inferior to the one we actually have. Of course, that conclusion has to be earned, not just asserted.

For the Record

What, then, is the best approach to constitutional interpretation? What approach does this book defend? What is the solution? (What rabbit might be pulled out of a hat?)

You might be disappointed to hear that my main goal is not to answer these questions. I am seeking to understand what those who disagree about theories of interpretation are actually disagreeing about, and offering an account of how to choose among competing theories. But just for the record, I agree with what Felix Frankfurter wrote in a private memorandum in 1953:[8]

> But the equality of the laws . . . is not a fixed formula defined with finality at a particular time. It does not reflect, as a congealed summary, the social arrangements and beliefs of a particular epoch. It is addressed to the changes wrought by time and not merely the changes that are the consequences of physical development. Law must respond to transformations of views as well as that of outward circumstances. The effects of changes in men's feelings for what is right and just is equally relevant in determining whether a discrimination denies the equal protection of the laws.

8. See Richard Kluger, *Simple Justice* (1977), 685.

True, the Constitution itself does not change over time (unless amended), but the meanings of its terms do change over time, not only because of changes in facts but also because of changes in values. Our system of constitutional law is a common-law process, in which assessments of particular cases, and social and judicial judgments over time, produce large-scale changes (even when the claim is one of restoration—a claim, by the way, that is often false). In the chapters that follow, I will attempt to explain these propositions, both by reference to interpretation in general and by reference to some concrete problems. How, for example, has the U.S. Constitution come to be understood to offer very broad protection of free speech? Or to forbid sex discrimination? The answers do not lie in recovery of some ancient wisdom.

At the same time, I believe that constitutional interpretation should be undertaken with close reference to the underlying goal of creating a *deliberative democracy*—a system that places a premium on reason-giving in the public domain (and hence on a *deliberative* democracy) and also on accountability to We the People (and hence on a deliberative *democracy*). A deliberative democracy prizes majority rule, but it is not simply majority rule. Majorities cannot simply do as they like simply because that is what they like to do. They must establish public-regarding justifications for their decisions. Reasons are essential. But a deliberative democracy is one of self-government, not bookishness or abstract theorizing. Self-government has certain preconditions, including protection of the franchise and a well-functioning system of freedom of expression.

With these points in mind, I am in emphatic agreement with John Hart Ely and Stephen Breyer insofar as they emphasize the need for a strong judicial role in protecting the preconditions for democratic self-government.[9] (This is not, by the way, a form of originalism.) The idea of deliberative democracy entails a significant role for federal courts in safeguarding political speech, the vote, and the democratic process as a whole. The role has always been important; it is crucial today. It also entails firm protection of those who are at a systematic disadvantage in the political process. That role, too, has always been important; it also is crucial today.

I believe all of these things, but (one more time, for emphasis) my main goal here is not to defend those beliefs. It is to defend some claims about the grounds on which you might or might not agree with them. My largest hope is that many readers might see, on reflection, that those claims are not wrong; and that they will recognize anew the (real) foundations of their own views about constitutional interpretation (and perhaps be willing to rethink them). If so, we will have a lot more clarity, not least because we will know what people are actually disagreeing about. With more clarity, we should have less yelling. And with more clarity, we might even be able to have more agreement on what is best about our constitutional order, which includes the creation of an ever-more-perfect union, with more in the way of democracy and more in the way of deliberation.

The Plan

This book consists of six chapters. Very briefly: Chapter 1 outlines the possible approaches; it is essentially a reader's guide. Chapters 2 and 3 explain why there are no quick wins here; no view can claim a victory from some noun (like "interpretation")

9. See Cass R. Sunstein, *The Partial Constitution* (1993).

or adjective (like "lawless"). Chapter 4 explains how we choose a theory of interpretation—and what reasonable people are disagreeing about. Chapter 5 focuses on traditionalism and its appeal, and why, in the end, it should be rejected.

In a bit more detail: Chapter 1 introduces the leading approaches to constitutional interpretation. Chapter 2 explains that there is nothing that interpretation just is—that we have a variety of conceptions of interpretation, and it is up to us which one to choose. Abstractions and generalities will not make that choice for us. Chapter 3 briefly investigates, and rejects, the claim that the oath of office entails a particular approach to interpretation. Because all judges take the oath, and because many people think that it has implications for the choice of theories of interpretation, I shall spend some time on it here. As we shall see, everything about the oath of office is interesting.

Chapter 4, the beating heart of the book, argues that fixed points, operating at various levels of abstraction, are crucial to the choice of a theory of interpretation. Chapter 5 turns to traditionalism, with particular reference to the Supreme Court's decision in the *Dobbs* case, which overruled *Roe v. Wade*. The central argument (or is it an article of faith?) is that the arc of history bends toward justice, which means that constitutional law should hesitate before turning long-standing practices into either a sword or a shield, and which means (above all) that improved moral understandings deserve to play a role in constitutional law. Chapter 6 is a cri de coeur, in the form of a brisk account of what, in my view, the U.S. Constitution should allow and forbid.

1

Theories of Interpretation

HERE ARE some words from the First Amendment to the U.S.
Constitution:

> Congress shall make no law respecting an establishment of
> religion, or prohibiting the free exercise thereof; or abridging
> the freedom of speech, or of the press.

Do these words protect blasphemy? Do they protect hate
speech? Do they protect false statements of fact, obscenity, or
commercial advertising? Do they forbid states from requiring
school prayer?

Here are some words from the Fourteenth Amendment:

> All persons born or naturalized in the United States, and sub-
> ject to the jurisdiction thereof, are citizens of the United
> States and of the State wherein they reside. No State shall
> make or enforce any law which shall abridge the privileges
> or immunities of citizens of the United States; nor shall any
> State deprive any person of life, liberty, or property, without
> due process of law; nor deny to any person within its juris-
> diction the equal protection of the laws.

Do these words forbid racial segregation? Do they protect the right to abortion? Do they protect polygamy? Do they protect the right to vote? Do they forbid affirmative action? Do they allow sex discrimination? Do they forbid maximum hour laws?

To answer such questions, we need to read the Constitution. To read the Constitution, we need to know the English language. But to understand what the Constitution means, an understanding of the English language is not nearly enough. We also need a theory of constitutional interpretation. This is so whether or not we have such a theory explicitly in mind. We might be oblivious to our own theory; we might think that the Constitution self-evidently forbids something or requires something. We might think, for example, that the Equal Protection Clause does not forbid discrimination on the basis of sex. If we think that, it must be because our theory of interpretation leads us to do so. We might deny that point. We might not think that we have a theory; the whole idea of a theory of interpretation might give us the willies or make us break out in hives. But if you think the Constitution has meaning, and that it resolves some dispute, you must be applying a theory of some kind.

Since the founding of the American Republic, there have been many such theories. My major question here is how to choose among them. Let us begin by considering, very briskly, the most prominent approaches. It is important to acknowledge that some of them are incomplete, and that some might overlap with others. For the sake of simplicity, and before we get to the details, we might note at the outset that most contemporary originalists embrace the original public meaning, and that most nonoriginalists embrace democracy-reinforcing judicial review, moral readings, or both. That is a major fault line in contemporary constitutional debates; it might well be *the* major fault line.

Textualism

Many people claim to be "textualists"; they insist on adhering to the text of the Constitution. They think that the text is binding, and they think it important as well as self-evident that judges must be faithful to it. Very few people claim *not* to be textualists; it is difficult to find people who insist on not adhering to the text of the Constitution, or who proudly claim, "I am not a textualist." Justice Elena Kagan famously said, "We are all textualists now." Who is not a textualist? Who was ever not a textualist?

In general, everyone agrees that the text of the Constitution is binding. Disagreements about the meaning of the Constitution typically occur because the text seems vague or ambiguous. We might agree that the text of the First Amendment, protecting "freedom of speech," is binding, without knowing whether the term includes falsehoods on social media, fraudulent advertisements, bribery, obscenity, or Holocaust denial. So why is it meaningful for people to insist that they are textualists, as if textualism is a kind of fighting faith, or a side in some sort of battle?

Here is one answer: Some people who claim to be textualists are conflating a commitment to following the text, as such, with a commitment to understanding the text *in certain ways*. If so, textualism, as they understand the term, is not only textualism; it is also something more controversial. Here is another answer: Some people might deny that they are textualists, not because they do not follow the text, but because they think that the text leaves all the hard questions open. That is a pretty good answer. At the very least, the text leaves a lot of hard questions open. The Second Amendment says this: "A well regulated Militia, being necessary to the security of a free State, the right of the people to keep and bear Arms, shall not be infringed." Does that mean that individuals have a right to carry guns in public, or not?

There are more subtle points. We may all be textualists now, but in a few cases, none of us may be textualists. The First Amendment says that "*Congress* shall make no law abridging the freedom of speech." It does not apply to the president, the Department of Justice, or the Department of Homeland Security. The Court reads the First Amendment as if it says, "The U.S. government shall not abridge the freedom of speech." Is that a mistake? (Short answer: No.) The Due Process Clause of the Fifth Amendment says this: "nor shall [any person] be deprived of life, liberty, or property, without due process of law." Does that text forbid racial segregation? As a matter of text, the answer is almost certainly no. The Court reads the Due Process Clause of the Fifth Amendment as if it says, "The federal government may not discriminate on the basis of race." Is that a mistake? (Same short answer.)

In addition, some historical work raises some real complications for textualists.[1] There is evidence that for the founders and ratifiers, the written Constitution was not all there was to "the Constitution." Some people, and perhaps many people, believed that "the Constitution" included a host of unwritten understandings and principles, which means that the text of the founding document did not exhaust the content of the Constitution. It is not clear that the writtenness of the Constitution suggested a sharp separation from prior understandings in

1. Jonathan Gienapp, *The Second Creation* (2018).

England, which saw "the Constitution" not in a written text but in background principles. As Jonathan Gienapp puts it, "Nothing about the sheer act of reducing constitutions to paper either signaled a clear break from prior constitutional assumptions or automatically clarified anything about those new constitutions' basic attributes."[2] In Gienapp's account, it was widely believed that the constitutional text did *not* exhaust constitutional principles.

In any case, the Ninth Amendment says this: "The enumeration in the Constitution, of certain rights, shall not be construed to deny or disparage others retained by the people." What does that mean, if we are textualists? What are these other rights? The text does not say. Any answer to that question will necessarily (I think) require us to go beyond textualism.

Semantic Originalism

Many people insist that the text of the Constitution must be interpreted in a way that is consistent with the original *semantic* meaning of its words.[3] Semantic originalism insists that in deciding on the meaning of words, we have to ask a question about history: What did the word mean, simply as a matter of the English language, at the time of ratification?

To see why semantic originalism might matter, consider these words from the Constitution:

> The United States shall guarantee to every State in this Union a Republican Form of Government, and shall protect each of them against Invasion; and on Application of the

2. Gienapp, *The Second Creation*, 22.

3. Lawrence B. Solum, The Unity of Interpretation, *B.U. L. Rev.* 90 (2010): 551, 572.

Legislature, or of the Executive (when the Legislature cannot be convened) against domestic Violence.

Pause, if you would, over the words "domestic Violence." In the twenty-first century, those words are usually taken to refer to "violence within the home." Would it be appropriate to understand the constitutional phrase in that way today? Would that make any sense? Would that be an admissible interpretation? Must the United States protect every state against violence within the home? (What would that even mean?)

Semantic originalists insist that the answer is obvious: *No.* They suggest that if the semantic meaning of words changes, interpreters of the Constitution must stick with the original semantic meaning and may not use the new one.

Or turn to these words: "The United States shall guarantee to every State in this Union a Republican Form of Government." Might it follow that the United States has to ensure that every state is run by the Republican Party? That every state is run by a form of government that meets with the approval of the Republican Party? Semantic originalists think that these questions answer themselves. The semantic meaning of "Republican Form of Government," at the time of ratification, is controlling (and it had nothing to do with the Republican Party).

According to semantic originalists, other constitutional terms—"the executive power," "equal protection," "due process of law"—cannot be interpreted to diverge from their semantic meaning at the time of the founding. Suppose that at some point in the future, "the executive power" is taken to include some new form of energy. If so, it would not follow that the Constitution has anything to say about that new form of energy.

But crucially, semantic originalists emphasize semantics alone. They believe that interpreters are not bound by the original public meaning of what the executive power specifically entailed, or of how far it reached. They insist that it would be wild for judges to depart from the original semantic meaning, but they agree that the original public meaning, as apart from semantics, need not be binding. At first glance, the distinction might seem elusive, but it really ought not to be. If we are semantic originalists, the word "equal" cannot mean a contemporary sugar substitute (even though there is one, "Equal"). But if we are semantic originalists, the word "equal" may or may not forbid discrimination on the basis of sex, even if it was not originally understood to forbid discrimination on the basis of sex.

For that reason, semantic originalism has something in common with textualism: It is not especially constraining. It would allow a host of new interpretations over time. For example, the semantic meaning of the phrase "the freedom of speech" could support very broad protection of speech—protection that goes far beyond historical understandings. Semantic originalists might be prepared to recognize a right to abortion, a right to same-sex marriage, even a right to polygamous marriage. Like textualism, semantic originalism does not have a lot of "bite." It leaves almost everything open.

Original Intentions

Some people embrace a form of originalism that is far more constraining than semantic originalism, and that is based on the idea of *authorial intentions*. For those who subscribe to this view, the meaning of constitutional provisions must be settled by asking a single question: *What did their authors intend?* If they intended the First Amendment not to protect blasphemy or commercial advertising, that is the end of the matter. If they intended the Equal Protection Clause to allow sex discrimination, then the Equal Protection Clause allows sex discrimination.

For example, Larry Alexander of the University of San Diego Law School writes that "given what we accept as legally authoritative, the proper way to interpret the Constitution . . . is to seek its authors' intended meanings—the same thing we do when we read a letter from Mom, a shopping list from our spouse, or instructions for how to assemble a child's toy made in China."[4] Walter Benn Michaels of the University of California at Berkeley goes further still: "In fact, however, you can't do textual interpretation without some appeal to authorial intention and, perhaps more controversially, you can't (coherently and nonarbitrarily) think of yourself as still doing textual interpretation as soon as you appeal to something beyond authorial intention—for example, the original public meaning or evolving principles of justice."[5] The basic idea is simple: Interpretation, including constitutional interpretation, necessarily requires us to seek the intention of the authors.

4. Larry Alexander, "Simple-Minded Originalism," San Diego Legal Studies Paper no. 08-067 (2008), available at http://papers.ssrn.com/sol3/papers.cfm?abstract_id=1235722.

5. See Walter Benn Michaels, A Defense of Old Originalism, *W.N.E. L. Rev.* 31 (2009): 21. For an analogous argument, see Steven Smith, *Law's Quandary* (2007); for an analogous argument with a focus on meaning rather than intentions, see Gary Lawson, On Reading Recipes . . . and Constitutions, *Geo L. J.* 85 (1997): 1823. For an instructive discussion, also with an emphasis on meaning, see Lawrence B. Solum, "Semantic Originalism," Illinois Public Law Research Paper no. 07-24 (2008), available at http://papers.ssrn.com/sol3/papers.cfm?abstract_id=1120244.

Michaels's claim is strong indeed, in part because of its claim of universality: "You can't do textual interpretation without some appeal to authorial intention." (As we shall see in chapter 2, that strong claim is wrong.) It is important to emphasize that in its contemporary form, originalism was born out of a commitment to authorial intention. In the 1980s and 1990s, the most influential originalists, most prominently Robert Bork, argued that the framers' intentions are binding—which meant that many of the left-of-center decisions of the Warren Court, including those protecting the right to privacy and the principle of one person, one vote, were fundamentally illegitimate. (I will note parenthetically here that in its modern form, originalism was born as a political movement, not only as a legal movement; it was a self-conscious response from the right to a set of Supreme Court decisions that pleased the left.) For a significant period of the time, original intentions originalism simply *was* originalism.

We should note that although original intentions originalism would seem to answer many questions, it could also leave important questions open. What was the original intention with respect to problems that the framers could not possibly have foreseen—as in, say, the use of military force by the president under the circumstances that followed the attacks of 9/11? What was the original intention with respect to new practices and technologies—say, wiretapping telephones, or using algorithms in the criminal justice system? What was the original intention with respect to regulation of speech on radio or television, or online? These are questions about how to apply the original intentions to new problems and situations. Perhaps we can answer such questions, reasoning by analogy. Perhaps speech on the radio or online is analogous to speech on the street, which would mean that efforts to regulate it must be

understood in exactly the same way. Perhaps wiretapping telephones is analogous to spying on homes. (The idea here is close
to Lawrence Lessig's concept of "translation" in constitutional
law; we will get to that in due course.)

But there are further questions. Was it the original intention
that "the freedom of speech" includes a set of specific results—
say, that political dissent is protected and that blasphemy is not
protected? Or was it the original intention that "the freedom of
speech" sets out a general principle whose particular meaning
would vary over time? Is that itself a historical question? Does
it have an answer? Is there a there there, as Gertrude Stein
doubted about Oakland?

Many people who emphasize original intentions would say
that the key questions are indeed historical. Those questions
may or may not be easy to answer. A possible approach would
be to say that while use of original intentions does not solve
every problem, it solves most problems—and that is all that can
be asked for a theory of interpretation. Is that correct? Does use
of the original intentions in fact solve most problems? As we
will see, that is not the easiest question to answer—in part
because history can be murky, in part because we need to decide at what level of generality to read the original intentions.

Original Public Meaning

Most contemporary originalists firmly reject original intentions
originalism. They object that the idea of "intentions" refers to
something subjective, to be found inside people's heads. They
do not think that in order to interpret the Constitution, we
should try to figure out the "intentions" of Alexander Hamilton,
John Jay, and James Madison. They also know that it can be
exceedingly challenging to figure out the "intentions" of large

groups of people (the "summing problem," as it is sometimes called).

They insist instead that the Constitution must be interpreted in a way that fits with its *original public meaning*. In their view, the original public meaning is objective, not subjective, and it does indeed make most constitutional questions easy. Original public meaning originalism is now ascendant; it is the preferred current form of originalism. Justice Antonin Scalia defended it. Justice Clarence Thomas subscribes to it, and so does Justice Neil Gorsuch. Justices Amy Coney Barrett, Samuel Alito Jr., and Brett Kavanaugh are keenly interested in it.

The original public meaning includes not only semantic meaning, but also the shared public context,[6] which offers various forms of "contextual enrichment."[7] We have seen that as a matter of semantics, many constitutional terms, such as "due process of law," could mean any number of things. But if we understand such phrases in their original context and in accordance with their original public meaning, they might mean just one thing. The Due Process Clause might mean, for example, that people must receive notice of a legal proceeding that is brought against them. Alternatively, it might mean that people have a right to a fair hearing. Alternatively, it might mean that the government cannot proceed against people unless it has good reasons for doing so. For public meaning originalists, meaning is settled by asking: *What was the public understanding at the time of ratification?*

---

6. This is the form of originalism discussed and challenged in Richard H. Fallon, The Chimerical Concept of Original Public Meaning, *Va. L. Rev.* 107 (2021): 1421.

7. See Lawrence B. Solum, The Public Meaning Thesis: An Originalist Theory of Constitutional Meaning, *B.U. L. Rev.* 101, no. 1953 (2020): 1983–88.

In Lawrence Solum's words, public meaning "is meaning for the public, the citizenry of the United States, and hence is related to the legal concept of 'ordinary meaning' as opposed to 'technical meaning.'"[8] Richard Fallon puts it this way: "Rather than defining the original public meaning as limited to minimally necessary (for intelligibility) or historically noncontroversial meaning, mainstream public meaning originalists posit that constitutional provisions' original public meanings consist of minimal meanings plus some further content that, they maintain, can also be discovered as a matter of historical and linguistic fact."[9] That is a complicated sentence. But let us underline the suggestion that constitutional meaning might be a product of an inquiry into history and thus a matter of *fact*.

You may or may not be drawn to public meaning originalism. It is more than interesting that as a young man, alert to the need for adaptation over time, James Madison appeared to reject originalism in all its forms and to seek a more flexible approach to constitutional interpretation. As Jonathan Gienapp puts it, young Madison "had assumed the Constitution was incomplete, partial, and in critical ways indeterminate."[10] He believed

8. See Solum, The Public Meaning Thesis, 1953. Solum also writes: "There are caveats and possible exceptions, but the general implication . . . is that the meaning of the constitutional text is a function of the conventional semantic meanings of the words and phrases as they are enriched and disambiguated by the public context of constitutional communication. In unusual cases, there can be divergence between the meaning of constitutional provisions that were intended by its Framers and public meaning" (2048). The word "unusual" deserves to be underlined. See Fallon, Chimerical Concept, 1427, for the argument that "original public meanings, in the sense in which originalists use that term, are insufficient to resolve any historically contested or otherwise reasonably disputable issue." Solum disagrees; see Solum, The Public Meaning Thesis.

9. Fallon, "Chimerical Concept," 1431.

10. Gienapp, *The Second Creation*, 332.

"that ongoing discussion and experiences would help make new meanings that would flesh out the unfinished edifice that he had helped construct."[11] In an important sense, young Madison believed in living constitutionalism, not public meaning originalism. For public meaning originalists, it is a nice question: If most people at the time agreed with Madison, then what becomes of public meaning originalism?

It is also more than interesting that in his later years, alert to the flexibility of semantic originalism and the risk of instability over time, Madison vigorously endorsed public meaning originalism. He did so in a plain effort to stabilize constitutional meaning.[12] The "meaning of a Constitution," Madison wrote, had to be "fixed and known" to ensure against "that instability which is incompatible with good government."[13] Madison no longer took "comfort in the new meanings generated through ongoing debates and adjudications"; instead he "sought to escape those processes, by freezing language in its place, by freezing its relentless dynamism."[14] A speculation: The elder Madison, seeing some of his life's work at risk, might well have had an interest in seeking to stabilize it.

Even if we share the elder Madison's goals and embrace public meaning originalism, we should acknowledge that, like original intentions originalism, it will not answer every question. New developments, new technologies, and new problems might present serious interpretive challenges. So might new

11. Gienapp, 332.

12. See Jonathan Gienapp, Written Constitutionalism, Past and Present, *Law and History Review* 39 (2021): 321, 327–33; regarding the "meaning of a Constitution," Madison took the opposite view during the debates over the Constitution (ibid., 333).

13. Gienapp, Written Constitutionalism, 329–30.

14. Gienapp, 332.

understandings and new values. Consider these words from *Brown v. Board of Education*:[15]

> In approaching this problem, we cannot turn the clock back to 1868, when the Amendment was adopted, or even to 1896, when *Plessy v. Ferguson* was written. We must consider public education in the light of its full development and its present place in American life throughout the Nation. Only in this way can it be determined if segregation in public schools deprives these plaintiffs of the equal protection of the laws.

These words are ambiguous. They might suggest, most modestly, a commitment to the original public meaning alongside a recognition that significant social changes are relevant to how, exactly, to understand that meaning. In other words, judges might have to follow the original public meaning but also understand that in the face of social changes, judgments about particular practices might have to shift. In line with the suggestion in *Brown*, racial segregation in public schools might not violate the Constitution at a time when public education did not play a significant role in American life, but it might violate the Constitution when public education is central to American life. For public meaning originalism, this is a complicated argument, but it is at least intelligible.

Alternatively, the passage in *Brown* might suggest, less modestly, a rejection of the original public meaning in light of social changes (such as the present place of public education in American life). Perhaps the Court should be understood to be saying that the Fourteenth Amendment is best taken as setting out abstract principles whose particular meaning is not frozen in time. We need to know whether to read the founding document

15. Brown v. Board of Education, 347 U.S. 483 (1954).

as containing such principles, capable of change over time, or instead as directing a set of concrete outcomes, not capable of change at all.

Some public meaning originalists say that this is a question of history and hence one of fact: Was the original public meaning a set of concrete outcomes or not? Some public meaning originalists emphasize the need to distinguish between "interpretation" and "construction," a distinction I take up in chapter 2.

Originalism as "Our Law"

Is originalism "our law"? If our legal system embraced originalism, perhaps we could simply say that we are originalists—full stop. William Baude and Stephen Sachs have urged that the American legal system turns out to be originalist.[16] As they put it, "the particular rules of our legal system happen to endorse a form of originalism."[17] On that view, we need not and should not attempt to choose a theory of interpretation as if we were Martians, deciding on the right theory for earthlings. Judges are earthlings, and more particularly they must respect the law of the system of which they are a part. Baude and Sachs think that originalism, in the sense of a commitment to the original public meaning, is the law of that system. They are public meaning originalists, but with a twist: They are public meaning originalists because (in their view) the system of American law is committed to public meaning originalism.

---

16. See William Baude and Stephen E. Sachs, Grounding Originalism, *Northwestern University Law Review* 113 (2019): 1455; William Baude and Stephen E. Sachs, The Law of Interpretation, *Har. L. Rev.* 130 (2017): 1079.

17. Baude and Sachs, Grounding Originalism, 1457.

Here is a simple way to make their point: If historians could show, for a fact, that the First Amendment was not understood to protect commercial advertising at the time of ratification, wouldn't the Supreme Court hesitate to protect commercial advertising? Baude and Sachs think that the answer is obviously yes. (I am not at all sure.)

To fill out the claim that our legal system is originalist, we would need, of course, to specify the form of originalism that our system is supposed to endorse. The distinctiveness of original law originalism lies in the claim that the American legal system already embraces originalism, which means that if we are asking what constitutional law is, there is just one answer: originalism.

Original Methods

Some people think that the Constitution must be interpreted in a way that is consistent with the ratifiers' views *about how it should be interpreted.*[18] On that view, judges need to follow the ratifiers' theory of interpretation.

If the ratifiers believed that judges should follow the original public meaning, judges must follow the original public meaning. If the ratifiers believed in original intentions originalism, we had better be original intentions originalists. If the ratifiers rejected originalism, we had better not be originalists (though our heads might spin a bit). If the ratifiers did not have a view about how the Constitution should be interpreted, we are stuck; we just have a gap.

---

18. See John McGinnis and Michael Rappaport, *The Good Constitution* (2013).

Original Expectations

Some people urge that the Constitution must be interpreted in a way that is consistent with the ratifiers' expectations about *how it should be interpreted in particular cases.*[19] Suppose, for example, that the ratifiers of the First Amendment had a narrow conception of "the freedom of speech," which would authorize the government to regulate blasphemy, obscenity, commercial advertising, and speech that it considered to be dangerous. Or suppose that the ratifiers of the Fourteenth Amendment believed that the states could engage in racial segregation or sex discrimination. Or suppose that the ratifiers of the First and Fourteenth Amendments did not think that they were banning mandatory school prayer. In any of these cases, current interpreters should be bound by their view.[20]

You might be inclined to think that original public meaning originalism and original expectations originalism are difficult to distinguish. Maybe they are even the same. It is true that they will often lead to the same conclusion, but those who believe in the original public meaning do *not* think that interpreters are bound by original expectations. The public might have expected, for example, that the First Amendment would not protect blasphemy, but the original public meaning of the First Amendment might be consistent with protection of blasphemy. For public meaning originalists, the original expectations are relevant but not controlling.

19. See Raoul Berger, *Government by Judiciary*, rev. ed. (1997); Christopher L. Eisgruber, *Constitutional Self-Government* (2001), 25–26 (understanding originalism as relying on original expectations).

20. On the expectations of the founding generation, see Jud Campbell, Natural Rights and the First Amendment, *Yale L. Rev.* 127 (2017): 246.

Protecting Democracy

Now let us turn to nonoriginalist approaches. John Hart Ely is the most prominent exponent of what is sometimes called "democracy-reinforcing judicial review." Ely understood himself as a defender of "the Warren Court"—the Supreme Court led by Chief Justice Earl Warren during the period from 1953 to 1969. The Warren Court interpreted the founding document to give broad protection to freedom of speech, to forbid racial segregation, to call for a principle of one person, one vote, and to confer an assortment of rights on criminal defendants. Whatever it was, the Warren Court was not an originalist court.

The Warren Court is the high-water mark of progressive constitutional law, or left-of-center constitutional law. For decades, it has operated as an inspiration and even a magnet for many citizens, lawyers, and law professors, giving a sense of what an aggressive Supreme Court, committed to certain understandings of liberty and equality, might do and be. For many others, it has been deeply unattractive, a warning, a signal of what an unelected Supreme Court, unmoored from the Constitution and in the grip of a particular ideology, might do and be. In some circles (though they are increasingly small), the Warren Court continues to orient thinking about the role of the judiciary and the proper approach to the Constitution. This is so even though, or perhaps because, the years of the Warren Court are the only period in U.S. history in which the Supreme Court regularly embraced progressive views about the Constitution, and understood the founding document to fit with an assortment of progressive ideals.

Many modern debates about constitutional interpretation are, in a sense, debates about the Warren Court. And while left-of-center practitioners and theorists have long admired the

Warren Court, many left-of-center practitioners and theorists now think that it was an anomaly, a curiosity of history, and that we should no longer see it as a guide. It is a nice question whether and in what sense they might be right.

Ely's dedication in his influential book *Democracy and Distrust* reads, "For Earl Warren. You don't need many heroes if you choose wisely."[21] Warren was not an originalist by any means. But on Ely's provocative account, he was thoroughly committed to democracy, and he understood the role of the Supreme Court by reference to that commitment. Ely's view can easily be seen as an elaboration of the most famous footnote in all of American constitutional law—footnote 4 in the *Carolene Products* case.[22] In that case, the Court emphasized its limited role in American government and said that it would be exceedingly reluctant to strike down state and federal legislation. At the same time, as a kind of qualification, footnote 4 said, in relevant part:

> It is unnecessary to consider now whether legislation which restricts those political processes which can ordinarily be expected to bring about repeal of undesirable legislation, is to be subjected to more exacting judicial scrutiny under the general prohibitions of the Fourteenth Amendment than are most other types of legislation [referring to "restrictions upon the right to vote"; "restraints upon the dissemination of information"; "interferences with political organizations"; and "prohibition of peaceable assembly"].
>
> Nor need we enquire whether similar considerations enter into the review of statutes directed at particular

21. John Hart Ely, *Democracy and Distrust: A Theory of Judicial Review* (1981).
22. United States v. Carolene Products, 304 U.S. 144, 152 n. 4 (1938).

THEORIES OF INTERPRETATION 39

religious, or national, or racial minorities; whether prejudice against discrete and insular minorities may be a special condition, which tends seriously to curtail the operation of those political processes ordinarily to be relied upon to protect minorities, and which may call for a correspondingly more searching judicial inquiry.

There is a lot there. The first paragraph just quoted points to the need for courts to play a strong role in protecting against deficits in democracy itself—as, for example, when the right to vote is compromised or when political speech is restricted. The second paragraph refers to the need for courts to play a strong role in protecting "discrete and insular minorities," which may not be able to protect themselves in politics. Ely offered a sustained elaboration of both points.

In Ely's view, the Constitution should be interpreted in a way that makes the democratic process work as well as possible, and that makes up for deficits in it. Above all, Ely urged that courts should vigorously protect the preconditions for self-government. One way to do that is to safeguard the franchise.[23] Ely insisted that courts should not allow public officials to entrench themselves. He believed that courts do well to strike down poll taxes and restrictions on access to the polls. The idea of one person, one vote does, on Ely's view, have a solid constitutional justification, whether or not it finds support in any form of originalism. On these counts, Ely's arguments might have a lot of contemporary resonance. They suggest that if states are making it harder for people to vote, or are not making it easier for people to vote, courts can legitimately strike down

23. See Ely, *Democracy and Distrust*; Stephen Breyer, *Active Liberty* (2006).

their actions. (You can fill in the details, depending on what is happening now, or on what has happened recently.)

To protect democracy, Ely also argued in favor of a vigorous judicial role in protecting political speech. If people are dissenting, even in the most disagreeable terms, the Supreme Court should protect them. For the same reason, Ely did not believe that the Constitution stands in the way of reasonable restrictions on campaign finance. In his view, such restrictions promote self-government; they do not undermine it.

Consistent with the second paragraph of footnote 4 quoted above, Ely urged as well that courts should protect those who are at a systematic disadvantage in the political process, including Black Americans and noncitizens. The Court was entirely right, in Ely's view, to strike down racial segregation in *Brown v. Board of Education*. The reason for the protection is to compensate for systematic imperfections or failures in democratic processes—to deliver the outcomes that we would see if those imperfections or failures did not exist, and hence to create a kind of democracy-reinforcing constitutional law. Ely approved of the idea of careful judicial scrutiny of any law that discriminates on the basis of race. But he added an important qualification. He had no trouble with affirmative action! On that issue, he believed, the democratic process can be trusted, because white Americans are not at a systematic disadvantage. Courts should not be suspicious of affirmative action programs, he thought, because white Americans would not be prejudiced against or hostile to themselves.

In general, Ely believed that the democratic process should have a great deal of room to maneuver, so long as the process is well-functioning. Ely had nothing to say in favor of *Roe v. Wade*. He was sharply critical of the right to privacy and of any judicial effort to identify and protect what judges saw as "fundamental values." (I will note parenthetically that in my view, Ely's book and enterprise are greatly underrated; he identified a kind of path not taken between 1980 and the present. It is more than intriguing to consider what a counterfactual world of constitutional law, rooted in Ely's views, might have looked like.)

Like his hero Warren, Ely did not embrace originalism, and indeed, he offered an extended critique of an early version of it (under the awkward name "interpretivism"). Still, he argued that his approach fit with the fundamental goals of the Constitution as a whole.

In a similar vein, Justice Stephen Breyer draws attention to the idea of "active liberty," understood to include participation in democratic processes, and he calls on courts to safeguard it.[24] He wants courts to protect the whole project of self-government. Breyer is not an originalist, though he does urge that his approach fits with, and attempts to implement, the most fundamental purposes of the founding document. You might well think of efforts to protect the democratic process as an effort to protect the broadest purposes of the Constitution as a whole—though originalists would wonder whether the relevant purposes are really being created rather than found.

Traditionalism

Many people, including many judges, are traditionalists; they think that constitutional interpretation should be undertaken with close reference to long-standing traditions. They are keen admirers of Edmund Burke, who deplored abstract theorizing about liberty and equality, and who argued in favor of careful attention to the beliefs and work of generations. If the question

---

24. See Breyer, *Active Liberty*.

involves privacy, religious freedom, gun rights, or access to court, traditionalists insist that judges should not make judgments on their own, or understand the Constitution by reference to their own views about what liberty or equality requires. Their own judgments are likely to be parochial (or foolish, or clueless). They do better to consult the wisdom of those who have built actual practices, as those practices have extended over periods of centuries. In a slogan: Practices yes, theories no.

Burke's key claim is that the "science of constructing a commonwealth, or reforming it, is, like every other experimental science, not to be taught a priori."[25] To make this argument, Burke opposes theories and abstractions, developed by individual minds, to traditions, built up by many minds over long periods. In a particularly vivid passage, Burke writes:[26]

> We wished at the period of the Revolution, and do now wish, to derive all we possess as *an inheritance from our forefathers*. . . . The science of government being therefore so practical in itself, and intended for such practical purposes, a matter which requires experience, and even more experience than any person can gain in his whole life, however sagacious and observing he may be, it is with infinite caution than any man ought to venture upon pulling down an edifice which has answered in any tolerable degree, for ages the common purposes of society, or on building it up again, without having models and patterns of approved utility before his eyes.

In the context of constitutional law, contemporary traditionalists urge that judges should interpret ambiguous

25. Edmund Burke, Reflections on the Revolution in France, in *The Portable Edmund Burke*, ed. Isaac Kramnick (1999), 416, 456–57.
26. Burke, "Reflections," 416, 456–57.

constitutional provisions by close reference to long-standing practices. In their view, democracy-reinforcing approaches are a form of hubris—an appeal to abstractions about self-government. In their view, the right to abortion is a concoction, a kind of barnacle on the Constitution (see chapter 5). Traditionalists do not like it when judges speak of evolving values or new understandings of liberty or equality. They cherish the wisdom of the past, not new thinking (about, say, same-sex marriage or the rights of criminal defendants).

Moral Readings

What if traditions are wrong? What if they are terrible? What if they are oppressive? Many people believe that the Constitution should be subject to a "moral reading," in the sense that its terms should be interpreted in a way that makes best moral sense of them, or that casts them in the best moral light.[27] We might, for example, understand freedom of speech far more broadly than the founding generation did, because that is the best moral reading of freedom of speech. In a sense, moral readers are at the opposite pole from traditionalists. They want to scrutinize traditions; they do not want to perpetuate them. They believe that traditions should be subject to the constraints of reason. They insist that the Supreme Court is a "forum of principle." They tend to be enthusiastic about constitutional bans on race and sex discrimination; they may have

27. See Ronald Dworkin, *Freedom's Law: The Moral Reading of the American Constitution* (1996). Some originalists do appear to be moral readers in practice. For a vivid illustration, see United States v. Vaello Madero, U.S. (2022) (Thomas, J., concurring in the judgment). For a general treatment, see Frank Cross, *The Failed Promise of Originalism* (2013). This fact does not, however, discredit originalism, though it might discredit (some) originalists.

no trouble with the right to choose abortion or the right to same-sex marriage. Actually they would be comfortable with much more.

On this view, developed most systematically by Ronald Dworkin, the question is not what "the freedom of speech" meant originally, or how our traditions have interpreted it, or how to understand it so as to protect democratic processes.[28] The question is *how to put that general principle in its most appealing form*. This is Dworkin's conception of law as "integrity."[29] We might understand "the freedom of speech" to include libel, blasphemy, obscenity, and commercial advertising, or we might not. We might understand the Equal Protection Clause to forbid discrimination on the basis of sex and sexual orientation, or we might not. Dworkin urges that judges (and the rest of us) need to discuss what makes the best moral sense out of the Constitution's "majestic generalities."

Dworkin's view did not come out of thin air; it has a long history, and it has many precursors and family members. In his book *The Least Dangerous Branch*, published in 1965, Yale law professor Alexander Bickel urged that because of their very insulation from the democratic politics, courts are in a unique position to discern moral principles and to apply them so as to give the right content to open-ended constitutional provisions.[30] Bickel was no originalist; when he wrote, originalism was not much on his viewscreen. But Bickel did worry about an excessive role for the federal courts in American democracy. He emphasized that judges are appointed through a political

28. See Dworkin, *Freedom's Law*. Dworkin wrote about the ideas in many places, and his views had many twists and turns; I do not mean to do a formal exegesis here.

29. See Ronald Dworkin, *Law's Empire* (1985).

30. See Alexander Bickel, *The Least Dangerous Branch* (1965).

process but not subject to electoral politics. In his view, judges are therefore in a unique position to develop principles, whether the issue involves freedom of speech, racial equality, or criminal justice. Dworkin agreed. In important ways, he followed in Bickel's footsteps.

Approaches to legal interpretation that some people describe as "purposive" or "teleological," emphasizing the Constitution's purposes and goals, can be seen as cousins to Dworkin's approach. Any effort to identify the purposes and goals of (for example) the right to freedom of speech might well turn out to be an effort to make the best constructive sense out of that right. How do we know the purposes of that right? Purposes are not like metal or wood; they are not something that you can feel or touch. If you say that the purpose of the First Amendment is to protect self-government, personal autonomy, or the marketplace of ideas, it is because you think that one or another of these formulations makes best sense out of that amendment. For better or for worse, you are a moral reader.

Something similar can be said about efforts to point to the importance of "translation" of constitutional provisions into new contexts, brilliantly developed by Lawrence Lessig.[31] How should we apply the restrictions on unreasonable searches and seizures to the internet? How can we "translate" the Constitution's grant of executive power to the president in an era in which the executive branch is so much bigger than it was at the founding? How can we tell what kind of control the president must have over (for example) the Environmental Protection Agency and the Federal Reserve Board? To translate something, including (for example) the system of separation of powers, you

31. See Lawrence Lessig, *Fidelity and Constraint* (2019).

might need to try to put it in the best constructive light. Of course, these various approaches could easily bear independent treatment, but for my purposes here, let us focus on the broad idea of moral readings.

You may or may not find the idea of moral readings of the Constitution appealing. If you do not, you might ask: Why on earth should we trust judges to make moral decisions? What gives them that right? What makes them good at that? Originalists and traditionalists press these questions. Dworkin's answer is not simple, but in brief, he contends that *there is no real alternative*—that judges *have* to make moral judgments, whatever they claim to be doing. In his view, originalism is a charade. A host of moral judgments must be made in order to specify the original meaning of constitutional phrases, even if those moral judgments lead us to allow elected officials to do as they think best. Thus Dworkin's words:[32]

> Rule by academic priests guarding the myth of some canonical original intention is no better than the rule by Platonic guardians in different robes. We do better to work, openly and willingly, so that the national argument of principle that judicial review provides is better argument for our part. We have an institution that calls some issues from the battleground of power politics to the forum of principle. It holds out the promise that the deepest, most fundamental conflicts between individual and society will once, someplace, finally, become questions of justice. I do not call that religion or prophesy. I call it law.

A number of people, including many judges, seem to follow Dworkin. Consider this passage from the Supreme

32. See Ronald Dworkin, The Forum of Principle, *N.Y.U. L. Rev.* 56 (1981): 469.

Court in its decision requiring states to recognize same-sex marriage:[33]

> The nature of injustice is that we may not always see it in our own times. The generations that wrote and ratified the Bill of Rights and the Fourteenth Amendment did not presume to know the extent of freedom in all of its dimensions, and so they entrusted to future generations a charter protecting the right of all persons to enjoy liberty as we learn its meaning. When new insight reveals discord between the Constitution's central protections and a received legal stricture, a claim to liberty must be addressed.

In addition to suggesting that originalism is a "myth," this is the basic claim of many of those who believe in moral readings. We "learn" the meaning of various principles, and constitutional law reflects what we learn. Some moral readers celebrate that fact. In their view, the arc of history bends toward justice, and judges should be part of history. Traditionalists, of course, decline to join the celebration. (In chapter 5, I will side with moral readers.)

You might think that moral readings are troublingly undemocratic. If so, you might be right. But Reva Siegel has emphasized that social movements are often important to the development of constitutional law.[34] In Siegel's account, such movements inform and shape constitutional conflict, and help account for the moral readings that we observe. If you are troubled by moral readings by unelected judges, Siegel's account might provide some comfort.

---

33. Obergefell v. Hodges, 576 U.S. 644, 663 (2015).

34. See, e.g., Reva Siegel, Constitutional Culture, Social Movement Conflict and Constitutional Change: The Case of the De Facto Era, *Cal. L. Rev.* 94 (2006): 1323.

Thayerism

In the late nineteenth century, Harvard law professor James Bradley Thayer wrote one of the most influential essays in the entire history of American law. Thayer argued in favor of a sharply limited role for courts in a democratic society.[35] He wanted judges to back off.

More specifically, Thayer urged that in the face of a constitutional challenge, all reasonable doubts should be resolved favorably to Congress, in the sense that the Constitution should be interpreted in a way that gives the political process maximum room to maneuver.[36] Justice Oliver Wendell Holmes offered one summary of the implications of Thayer's position (and wholeheartedly embraced it): "If my fellow citizens want to go to Hell I will help them. It's my job."[37] Thayer was less pithy and more optimistic. He did not speak of going to hell. He had faith in the democratic process. Because of Thayer's influence and the large shadow he casts over all of constitutional law, let's spend a little time in his company.

Thayer began his essay with a large puzzle: "How did our American doctrine, which allows to the judiciary the power to declare legislative Acts unconstitutional, and to treat them as null, come about, and what is the true scope of it?"[38] In Thayer's

---

35. See James Bradley Thayer, The Origin and Scope of the American Doctrine of Constitutional Law, *Har. L. Rev.* 7 (1893): 129. A valuable discussion of Thayer's motivations, emphasizing what he sees as Thayer's political conservatism and desire to activate political focus on combating ill-considered progressivism, is Mark Tushnet, Thayer's Target: Judicial Review or Democracy?, *Nw.U. L. Rev.* 88 (1993): 9.

36. See Thayer, "Origin and Scope," 43.

37. Mark De Wolfe Howe, ed., *Holmes-Laski Letters* (1953), 249.

38. Thayer, "Origin and Scope," 129.

view, this power cannot be justified by the mere fact that the Constitution is written or in the oath of office (taken up in chapter 3):

> So far as the grounds for this remarkable power are found in the mere fact of a constitution being in writing, or in judges being sworn to support it, they are quite inadequate. Neither the written form nor the oath of the judges necessarily involves the right of reversing, displacing, or disregarding any action of the legislature or the executive which these departments are constitutionally authorized to take, or the determination of those departments that they are so authorized.[39]

The remarkable practice of judicial review, as Thayer called it, was a product not of logic but of experience, and in particular a product of our political experience before the Revolutionary War.[40] (Remember Concord?) Great Britain had an external sovereign; the United States did not. In the United States, We the People are sovereign. Thayer put it this way: "Our own home population in the several States were now their own sovereign. So far as existing institutions were left untouched, they were construed by translating the name and style of the English sovereign into that of our new ruler,—ourselves, the People."[41] Judges enforced the precepts of the Constitution in the interest of protecting the sovereignty of the people themselves against public officials.

This is what happened. But as Thayer saw it, the practice of judicial review was hardly inevitable, and it was *not* clearly mandated by the Constitution itself. Thayer found it "instructive to

39. Thayer, 130.
40. Thayer, 130.
41. Thayer, 131.

see that this new application of judicial power was not univer-
sally assented to. It was denied by several members of the federal convention, and was referred to as unsettled by various
judges in the last two decades of the last century."[42] In the
founding period, the power of judicial review was sharply disputed. As that power emerged and became entrenched, its
scope was to determine whether the Constitution was violated
by some legislative enactment. In a crucial passage, Thayer said
that such questions

> require an allowance to be made by the judges for the vast and
> not definable range of legislative power and choice, for that
> wide margin of considerations which address themselves only
> to the practical judgment of a legislative body. Within that
> margin, as among all these legislative considerations, the con-
> stitutional law-makers must be allowed a free foot.[43]

Under the right approach, "an Act of the legislature is not to
be declared void unless the violation of the constitution is so
manifest *as to leave no room for reasonable doubt.*"[44] Thayer urges
that this idea was established early and in fact became entrenched by 1811.[45] What was necessary, for invalidation, was a
clear and unequivocal violation of the Constitution. As Thayer
understood it, courts "can only disregard the Act when those
who have the right to make laws have not merely made a

42. Thayer, 132.

43. Thayer, 132.

44. Note that this claim is not the same as the "rational basis" test for reviewing
legislation. The rational basis test is rooted in *the Court's independent interpretation* of
the requirements of various constitutional provisions; in the Court's view, what is
required is a rational basis (no more and no less).

45. Thayer, Origin and Scope, 140.

mistake, but have made a very clear one,—so clear that it is not open to rational question."

Suppose, for example, that Congress enacts aggressive minimum wage and maximum hour laws, and that companies argue that such laws violate the Constitution. Thayer would not be sympathetic to their arguments. Or suppose that Congress prohibited abortion or same-sex marriage, required affirmative action, or imposed the death penalty. Here as well, Thayerians would be strongly inclined to uphold those actions. The reason is that in these cases, and countless others, the constitutional question is at least "open to rational question," which means that courts must not strike legislation down.

Thayerism has a kind of neutrality—perhaps an impressive neutrality. It calls for judicial modesty, whether the measure in question is challenged by the left or by the right. But it is revealing that in the long history of American law, it is exceedingly difficult to find consistent or across-the-board Thayerians. Holmes himself may have been the closest. He voted in favor of minimum wage and maximum hour laws, and he insisted that legislatures can adopt whatever economic theories they like: "The Fourteenth Amendment does not enact Mr. Herbert Spencer's Social Statics."[46] Holmes also voted in favor of compulsory sterilization laws, suggesting that legislatures have a lot of room to maneuver: "Three generations of imbeciles are enough."[47] Felix Frankfurter, who idolized Holmes, also idolized Thayer, and was mostly a Thayerian—which got him in a lot of trouble with the political left (with whom he agreed as a matter of politics). For example, Frankfurter voted to uphold compulsory flag salute laws, and he would have allowed a host of restrictions on freedom of speech.

46. Lochner v. New York, 198 U.S. 45, 75 (1905) (Holmes, J., dissenting).
47. Buck v. Bell, 274 U.S. 200, 207 (1927).

In the modern era, however, there are no consistent Thayerians. Some left-of-center justices, such as Justices Ruth Bader Ginsburg and Stephen Breyer, have been Thayerians with respect to the Second Amendment—but not with respect to sex discrimination. Some right-of-center justices, such as Justices Clarence Thomas and Antonin Scalia, have been Thayerians with respect to abortion—but not with respect to the Second Amendment. If we are originalists, of course, we might refuse to be Thayerians; we will follow the original meaning (and be Thayerians only when the original meaning, or something in the public understanding at the time of ratification, directs us to be). If we are traditionalists, we might refuse to be Thayerians; everything might depend on the content of the traditions, and on how clear they are. Those who believe in democracy reinforcement will be inclined to reject Thayerism when democracy is at risk but will uphold legislation much of the time. (Ely is a case in point; he was often something like a Thayerian.) Moral readers might be Thayerian when their preferred moral reading of the Constitution calls for it. Many moral readers will be unlikely to uphold sex discrimination, but they might have no trouble with restrictions on commercial advertising (it all depends on their moral readings, of course). Justice Ruth Bader Ginsburg was often a moral reader, and she was no Thayerian.

These points suggest that for all its importance, the Thayerian approach is radically incomplete. To know whether a constitutional violation is clear, we need a theory of interpretation to help us to understand what the Constitution means. We could imagine Thayerian textualists, who would uphold statutes and regulations against constitutional challenge unless there is, beyond a reasonable doubt, a violation of the text of the founding document. We could also imagine Thayerian originalists, who would uphold statutes and regulations against constitutional attack unless the violation of the document, on the correct originalist reading, was clear.

To be sure, originalists would want to ask some hard questions about Thayerism, above all this one: Is it part of, or consistent with, the original public meaning? For originalists, Thayerism would seem to stand or fall on the answer to that question. While it might be challenging to answer that question as a matter of history, the consequences of Thayerian originalism are not obscure. Under Thayerian originalism, the First Amendment would not forbid blasphemy laws.[48] Under Thayerian originalism, states could segregate public schools on the basis of race, and so could Congress. Under Thayerian originalism, there would probably be no "substantive due process" under either the Fifth or the Fourteenth Amendment, which means that states could ban contraception, prohibit consensual sexual practices, and forbid same-sex marriage.[49]

We could easily imagine moral reader Thayerians, who would believe that the Constitution should be given a moral reading, but also that courts should uphold the decisions of the democratic branches unless the violation of the (best) moral reading was very clear. For example, nonoriginalist Thayerians might believe that the best moral reading of the Equal Protection Clause forbids affirmative action, but also that the issue is not straightforward, which would mean that affirmative action programs should be upheld.

We could even imagine Thayerians of a more extreme sort, who would uphold legislation if, under *any* reasonable theory

48. Note, Blasphemy Laws and the Original Meaning of the First Amendment, *Har. L. Rev.* 135 (2021): 689.

49. Lawrence B. Solum and Max Crema, The Original Meaning of 'Due Process of Law' in the Fifth Amendment, *Va. L. Rev.* 108 (2022): 447.

of constitutional interpretation, it is not unconstitutional beyond a reasonable doubt. For such Thayerians, the best approach would be to use the most permissive theory of interpretation and to ask if the relevant legislation is unambiguously inconsistent with that theory. In general, textualism is probably the most permissive approach to interpretation, in the sense that the constitutional text, by itself, often allows reasonable doubts with respect to a very wide range of possible understandings.

At some points in American history, Thayerism has had a strong appeal to the political right. During the ascendancy of the Warren Court, many conservatives seemed Thayerian. They rejected "judicial activism," which they found in judicial rulings striking down the actions of the democratic branches; consider the desegregation decisions, the *Miranda* ruling, *Roe v. Wade*, and the idea of one person, one vote. Conservatives wanted courts to be more deferential and hence more Thayerian. In recent decades the left has shown far more interest in Thayerism, in evident response to rulings from the Supreme Court that seem, to the left, to be unfortunate or outrageous. On numerous occasions, the left has explored ways to limit the place of the Supreme Court in American life.

One version of left-of-center Thayerism is a belief in "popular constitutionalism," which sometimes takes the form of a rejection of the power of judicial review altogether. For some people who endorse popular constitutionalism, the Supreme Court should defer to the constitutional judgments of the political branches, which would mean that their actions would not be struck down. Campaign finance restrictions, gun control laws, affirmative action programs, restrictions on commercial advertising, wealth taxes—all these, and many more, would be upheld. With respect to the separation of powers, Nikolas Bowie and Daphna Renan have argued in favor of a more deferential role for the Supreme Court, one that would require courts to accept a wide range of political accommodations.[50] The argument offered by Bowie and Renan does not have a clear political valence, but it can be seen to fit with a significant strand in progressive legal thought, and it is broadly Thayerian.

There is a background point in support of left-wing Thayerism: It is often urged that as a matter of history, and as a matter of the likely future, the Supreme Court will reflect the political views of the powerful and the wealthy (as befits the fact that the justices are members of a political elite—lawyers who may have a strong commitment to the status quo). For those who embrace left-of-center Thayerism, or the abolition of judicial review, the most revealing judicial decisions are those

- striking down maximum hour and minimum wage laws;
- protecting the right to possess guns;
- banning affirmative action programs;
- striking down campaign finance regulation;
- protecting commercial advertising;
- jeopardizing the Affordable Care Act; and
- forbidding regulation designed to protect safety, health, and the environment.

To say the least, such Thayerians doubt that democracy reinforcement is likely to be the wave of the future. If inadequate democracy is the problem, they think, the Supreme Court is hardly the solution. And such Thayerians are deeply skeptical of the idea of moral readings, which, they believe, are reflections, often hidden, of an identifiable political agenda,

50. See Nikolas Bowie and Daphna Renan, The Separation of Powers Counter-revolution, *Yale L. Rev.* 131 (2021): 2020.

associated with the political right. When the Supreme Court purports to be originalist and reflects right-of-center values, Thayerians might be inclined to lament: There are some moral readings for you.

Common-Law Constitutionalism

In England and the United States, common-law courts develop principles of contract law, property law, and tort law not by reference to some authoritative text, but on a case-by-case basis. They develop governing principles after careful engagement with the facts of individual disputes. Courts might decide, for example, that someone does not have to comply with a contractual obligation (say, to complete construction work) if there was an earthquake during the week of the due date. Then courts might be asked whether someone has an obligation to comply with a contractual obligation if there was a snowstorm. They decide whether the principle that covers the earthquake case also covers the snowstorm case.

Is constitutional law like that? Some people think so. They believe the document contains abstractions ("freedom of speech," "equal protection," "due process") that are best taken as the foundation for a process of case-by-case judgment, in which the document's text and the original public meaning do not have a decisive role. They may not even be particularly important.[51]

On this view, elaborated most prominently by David Strauss, judges typically reason from one case to another, perhaps with the assistance of low-level principles; they do not spend a lot of time with the Constitution's text or with the original

51. David A. Strauss, *The Living Constitution* (2010).

meaning. They might decide, for example, that the Constitution protects the right to use contraceptives within marriage. Then they might be asked to decide whether the Constitution protects the right to use contraceptives outside of marriage. Then they might be asked to decide whether the Constitution protects the right to choose abortion. Then they might be asked to decide whether the Constitution protects the right to same-sex marriage. Whether the case involves privacy, religion, speech, or discrimination, judges reason by analogy; they go from one ruling to another, developing principles—typically at a low level of ambition ("liberty includes the right to make choices about contraception within marriage")—that they might or might not expand. In this common-law process, the text of the Constitution, taken as such, is very much in the background. To be sure, judges must ordinarily be faithful to the text, but as we have seen, it does not decide hard cases. The real work is done by case-by-case decision making, developing and refining the relevant principles. What such decision making entails or involves is itself a keenly interesting question; the process of analogical reasoning raises many questions and problems. The only point is that American constitutional law is a lot more like Anglo-American common law than we tend to think.

It should be clear that common-law constitutionalism might go in any number of directions. Through case-by-case judgments, we could end up with a very broad right of privacy or with no right of privacy at all. Through case-by-case judgments, we could end up allowing almost all affirmative action programs or forbidding almost every affirmative action program. Through case-by-case judgments, we could end up with a ban on capital punishment or with few restrictions on capital punishment. Those who celebrate common-law constitutionalism do not dispute this point. Instead they argue that the process of case-by-case reasoning, focused on details and respectful of precedent, has large advantages over more top-down approaches, invoking abstract theories about (for example) liberty or equality, or the broad power of the president.

In this way, common-law constitutionalists have a real overlap with traditionalists. The difference is that the common-law constitutionalists can and often do believe in moral progress. They may be quite comfortable with processes of case-by-case judgment that end up repudiating traditions (as, for example, by requiring states to stop discriminating on the basis of sex or to recognize same-sex marriages). In this light, it should be clear that common-law constitutionalists often march hand in hand with moral reasoners. The difference is that common-law constitutionalists are cautious about ambitious theorizing from the Supreme Court. They prefer the humility and the incrementalism of the common-law process.

Common-Good Constitutionalism

Some people urge that the Constitution should be interpreted in a way that is consistent with principles of "the common good," as those principles have been understood and elaborated over time.[52] On this view, originalism is a modern concoction, one that does not, ironically enough, fit with the values or the approach of the founding generation. Adrian Vermeule describes a commitment to the common good, fitting with longstanding traditions, that may or may not "fall out" of the original public meaning of the text but that nonetheless should and often does play a crucial role in contemporary constitutional

52. See Adrian Vermeule, *Common Good Constitutionalism* (2022).

law. Vermeule argues that common-good constitutionalism actually conforms to the views of the founding generation. With historical support, he suggests that originalism, in its modern form, is not reflective of what that generation thought. Recall here the words of the Ninth Amendment, which raises many puzzles but which might be taken to support common-good constitutionalism: "The enumeration in the Constitution, of certain rights, shall not be construed to deny or disparage others retained by the people."

At the level of method, Vermeule borrows heavily from Dworkin; he favors moral readings (and thinks them essentially inevitable). But Vermeule insists that common-good constitutionalism offers the *better* moral readings, and that Dworkin's inclination to favor progressive readings, associated with the contemporary political left, does not. We might be inclined to see an overlap between traditionalism and common-good constitutionalism. Insofar as traditionalism points to long-standing understandings of the common good, the two tend to merge in practice. But common-good constitutionalism can be taken to have a more substantive orientation, focused as it is on specific ideas and ideals associated with the common good.

———

We now have had a tour of the horizon, in the form of a catalog of the leading theories of constitutional interpretation. It should also be clear that if one adopted a particular theory, one's approach to constitutional law will be powerfully oriented by it.

Thayerism would mean that the Supreme Court would uphold nearly everything. Racial segregation would be fine, and so would be affirmative action. Sex discrimination would be fine, and so would be campaign finance regulation. Restrictions on commercial advertising would be fine, and so would be restrictions on obscenity. If we embraced democracy-reinforcing judicial review, we might not have a right of privacy, but we would have robust safeguards against restrictions on the franchise, and political gerrymandering would probably be policed by the Supreme Court. If we embraced certain forms of originalism, our constitutional order would be different from what it now is and in some ways barely recognizable. The national government could freely discriminate on the basis of race and sex. It could also forbid speech that it considered to be dangerous.

How, exactly, does that matter to our institutions and to our rights? To our choice of theories of interpretation? We will get to that in chapter 4, but let us turn first to a large issue: freedom and constraint.

2

The Inevitability of Choice

WHICH APPROACH IS BEST? How should we go about answering that question? Is that even the right question? In this chapter, I aim to show that all of the contested approaches are options for us, and that none of them is mandatory (with the possible exception of textualism). We need to justify our choice, and we must do so on grounds that are external to the Constitution itself. We cannot read any of them off the founding document.

For some people, this will be a contentious claim. They believe that the Constitution *must* be interpreted in their preferred way. They insist that the very idea of interpretation requires judges to adopt their own preferred method of construing the founding document. This view is especially pervasive among originalists, though some version of it can be found among nonoriginalists as well, and though some originalists do emphasize that their preferred approach must be justified on some external grounds (involving, for example, legitimacy, stability, or the rule of law).

My central claim in this chapter is that in the context of constitutional law, there is nothing that interpretation "just is." Among the reasonable alternatives, no approach to constitutional interpretation is required or self-justifying. Any approach must be defended on some ground—not asserted as part of what interpretation requires by its nature. Whatever their preferred approach, both judges and lawyers must rely on evaluative judgments of their own. Nonetheless, they sometimes claim that their own approach is *necessary*, in the sense that they have no choice but to adopt it if they are to engage in interpretation at all. That claim is a recipe for confusion. But it is worse than that. It is a recipe for unearned dogmatism.

As we shall see, my central argument means that judges (and others) have a degree of freedom: They get to choose their own theory of interpretation. No one has made their choice for them. But freedom is not a blank check or a kind of license. Any theory must be defended on the ground that it will make our constitutional order better rather than worse. (How can we think well about that? That is the topic of chapter 4.)

It is true that some imaginable practices cannot count as interpretation at all. The text matters. If judges do not show fidelity to authoritative texts, they cannot claim to be interpreting them. But a text is not identical to its original meaning. Without transgressing the legitimate boundaries of interpretation, judges can show fidelity to a text in a variety of ways. Within those boundaries, the choice among possible approaches depends on a claim about what makes our constitutional system best.

Importantly, this conclusion does not, by itself, immediately rule out any of the established approaches. But it does establish the terrain on which the debates must be undertaken.[1]

1. The valuable discussion in Lawrence B. Solum, The Positive Foundations of Formalism: False Necessity and American Legal Realism, *Har. L. Rev.* 127 (2014): 2464, can be understood to sketch a consequence-focused argument for originalism

My goal in this chapter is to defend these conclusions. The reason they need defending is simple: many people believe that they are wrong. But as we explore some of the contested theories described in chapter 1, we will see in each case that they have to be justified on the ground that they will make our constitutional order better rather than worse. It is not enough to stomp one's feet.

Original Intentions

Recall original intentions originalism: In interpreting the meaning of words, we ask about authorial intentions. (I use the term "author" to include speakers as well as writers.) Some people think that is what it means to interpret words; they believe that theirs is the only reasonable way to interpret any text, including the Constitution. It is a preposterous claim; let's see why.

It is true that in ordinary life, we tend to interpret words in this way. If a friend says to you, "Meet me at my favorite restaurant," you will probably ask yourself what, exactly, she has in mind. You will not ask which restaurant you like best, or which restaurant is preferred by your favorite restaurant critic. It is consistent with ordinary usage to say that in most conversational settings, interpretation of people's words amounts to an effort to figure out their intentions. Of course, this conclusion invites attention to context and purposes, not just words. If a friend makes some kind of linguistic error, you would not want to hold her to those words. If she says, "Meet me in New Jersey," when she clearly means, "Meet me in New York," you would not meet her in New Jersey. But when you depart from her words,

---

and plain-meaning approaches to legal texts. See also John O. McGinnis and Michael B. Rappaport, *Originalism and the Good Constitution* (2013).

it is because you are trying to figure out what she had in mind. As we have seen, some people think that legal interpretation is not fundamentally different. In their view, a form of originalism, based on the idea of authorial intention, is built into the concept of interpretation.

It is true that we could *define* legal interpretation in this way. But if we did, the definition would be just a stipulation, and it would not be based on the necessary meaning of the term. Let us suppose that in ordinary conversation, most people understand the idea of interpretation to involve a search for authorial intentions. Even in that context, such an understanding is not mandatory. We could imagine the view that interpretation involves a search for public meaning rather than authorial intentions—that we should try to understand (for example) which restaurant is generally agreed to be the best, not the restaurant that is our friend's personal favorite. But it is certainly sensible to say that in conversation, we ask about intentions. If this is indeed sensible, it is for a *pragmatic* reason; the goal of the particular communication will not be met if we do not.

When a friend asks me to meet her or to do something for her, I am likely to ask about her intentions because I want to meet her or to do as she would like. If my friend says that we should "meet at the best museum in town," I will likely ask what she meant by those words. It is imaginable, of course, that she wants me to do a little work and to see which museum the experts like best—but if so, I am still trying to follow her subjective intentions. If interpretation entails that practice, it is because in the relevant context, that is the best way to understand the term.

The same things might be said about communication within some hierarchical organization. If a supervisor tells an employee what to do, it is right to think that in ordinary circumstances, the employee ought to ask: "What, exactly, did my supervisor mean by that?" (The qualification "in ordinary circumstances" is necessary because even subordinates sometimes ask about something other than speaker's intentions; everything depends on the role of the subordinate, some of whom might have a different or less deferential role.) The employee asks this question, if he does, for pragmatic reasons. Employees should generally follow the instructions of their supervisors, and the practice of following instructions in hierarchical organizations usually calls for close attention to the supervisors' subjective intentions. It is not wrong to say that in some contexts, interpretation of the instructions of a supervisor "just is" an effort to elicit and follow subjective intentions—not in the sense that this understanding of interpretation is inevitable or strictly mandatory, but in the sense that it captures how most people use the term in such contexts. If that is true, it is because this understanding of interpretation makes the supervisor–employee relationship work best.

A possible response would be that, at least in many contexts, it is not even possible to interpret people's words without making some kind of judgment about the author's intentions. On this view, the idea of meaning depends on some such judgment, and it is incoherent without it. In the legal context, this claim is plainly false, for reasons that are elaborated below.[2] For the

2. I think that it is false even in ordinary communications. Suppose that you look up at a pattern of clouds in the sky. To your surprise, the pattern spells out the word "God." Whether or not you have faith, you will have no hesitation identifying that word. Conventions about language may be sufficient for the identification, suggesting the possibility that we can understand the meanings of words by reference to those conventions, without necessarily making judgments about author's intentions. This example is contested in Steven Smith's *Law's Quandary* (2004).

moment, let us turn to a different understanding of originalism—
not yesterday's originalism, but today's.

Original Meaning

We have seen that the most committed contemporary originalists, led by Justice Scalia and now including Justices Clarence
Thomas and Neil Gorsuch, believe that what matters is the
original public meaning of the document, not intentions at
all.[3] In *District of Columbia v. Heller*,[4] for example, Justice Scalia wrote that in "interpreting [the Second Amendment], we are
guided by the principle that '[t]he Constitution was written to
be understood by the voters; its words and phrases were used
in their normal and ordinary as distinguished from technical
meaning.'" Justice Scalia meant to point to the understanding
of We the People, not that of specialists (including lawyers!).
As he put it, "Normal meaning may of course include an idio-
matic meaning, but it excludes secret or technical meanings
that would not have been known to ordinary citizens in the
founding generation."[5]

At times, originalists themselves have argued fiercely about
whether the original public meaning, or instead the original
intentions, should be taken as authoritative—a point that in
itself suggests that interpretation, to qualify as such, need not
be focused on one or the other, and that reasonable people can
argue about the best way to interpret words. We have seen that

---

3. See District of Columbia v. Heller, 554 U.S. 570 (2008). Grice similarly distinguishes between "speaker's meaning" and "sentence meaning." See H. P. Grice,
Utterer's Meaning, Sentence-Meaning, and Word Meaning, *Foundations of Language*
4 (1968): 225.

4. 554 U.S. 570 (2008).

5. 554 U.S. 570 (2008).

those who focus on original public meaning, now very much in the ascendancy, argue that meaning is objective, not subjective. In their view, what matters is the standard understanding among the Constitution's ratifiers, not what the authors intended. After all, the ratifiers ("We the People"), and not the authors, turned the Constitution into law. Rejecting subjective intentions, Justice Holmes wrote, "We do not inquire what the legislature meant; we ask only what the statutes mean."[6]

My goal is not to take a stand on which form of originalism is best or most coherent (if I had to pick, I would pick original public meaning), or to suggest that the original meaning must be taken as fixed and binding (I do not believe that!). It is only to insist that the internal debates about what originalism requires are pretty good evidence that attention to subjective intentions is not built into the very idea of interpretation. If some intelligent originalists call for attention to intentions, and other intelligent originalists call for attention to the public meaning, it would seem unlikely that the abstract idea of interpretation, standing by itself, requires one rather than the other.

The Only Real Question: What Makes Our System Best?

Is it plausible to say that interpretation *necessarily* entails a search for the original public meaning, as some judges seem to think? Not at all.

Larry Alexander is right to suggest that interpretation often involves an inquiry into intentions rather than public meaning. We could at least imagine a form of textualism that inquires

6. Oliver Wendell Holmes, The Theory of Legal Interpretation, *Har. L. Rev.* 12 (1899): 417.

about *contemporary* meaning—thus calling for adherence to the current, rather than the historical, meaning of the constitutional text. More plausibly, we could imagine what we have already seen, which is a commitment to semantic originalism *without a commitment to the original public meaning*; many judges seem to embrace that view, which cannot be ruled out of bounds by the very idea of interpretation.

As I have noted, some of those who insist on fidelity to the original public meaning do not insist that their own view is compelled by the very idea of interpretation. To their credit, they suggest that their own approach would lead to a better system of constitutional law.[7] They focus, that is, not on the claim that their theory is the only possible way to read the Constitution, but on showing that their theory would make the constitutional order better rather than worse. Lawrence Solum, the most careful expositor and defender of originalism, sometimes argues to this effect. He notes plainly that "originalists must make normative arguments for originalism."[8] Most of those normative arguments are arguments about the good consequences for the American constitutional system, broadly conceived, that would follow from originalism. Solum himself thinks that public meaning originalism is the best way of promoting the rule of law, avoiding (judicial) tyranny, increasing

---

7. Lawrence B. Solum, *The Constraint Principle* (2018), 81, available at https://ssrn .com/abstract=2940215, urges that "a deep consequentialist argument is not appropriate as the sole justification for a constitutional theory in a society characterized by the fact of pluralism." I do not think that Solum and I disagree on anything here; his points about the rule of law and legitimacy, which he deems not to be consequentialist, fall within what I am treating as a large tent. Compare Amartya Sen's broad conception of welfarism in his "Utilitarianism and Welfarism," *Journal of Philosophy* 76 (1979): 463.

8. See Solum, *The Constraint Principle*, 81.

stability, and fulfilling other goals. I do not agree with him, but in an imaginable world he is right, and I think that Solum has correctly identified the territory on which reasonable people might differ. Indeed, it is intriguing to see some originalists making arguments of Solum's sort while also arguing, implausibly, that their view is compelled by the very idea of interpretation, or can in some sense be read off the Constitution or its underlying logic.

For example, Justice Scalia makes both kinds of arguments. His own defense of originalism, as a "lesser evil," focuses a great deal on what would make the American constitutional order (or any constitutional order) better rather than worse. Justice Scalia is much concerned about the risks associated with judicial discretion; he thinks that nonoriginalist approaches, and any form of "living constitutionalism," will effectively license judges to do whatever they want. In a democracy, how can that be a good thing? Justice Scalia contends that if judges adhere to original meaning, the relevant risks will be diminished, because judges will be constrained.[9] Those are fair points; any approach to constitutional interpretation must contend with them.

But compare this complicated passage, in which Justice Scalia speaks more grandly:[10]

> The principal theoretical defect of nonoriginalism, in my view, is its incompatibility with the very principle that legitimizes judicial review of constitutionality. Nothing in the text of the Constitution confers upon the courts the power to inquire into, rather than passively assume, the

9. Antonin Scalia, Originalism: The Lesser Evil, *U.Cinn. L. Rev.* 57 (1989): 849, 854.

10. Scalia, Originalism, 849, 854.

constitutionality of federal statutes. That power is, however, reasonably implicit because, as Marshall said in *Marbury v. Madison*, (1) "[i]t is emphatically the province and duty of the judicial department to say what the law is," (2) "[i]f two laws conflict with each other, the courts must decide on the operation of each," and (3) "the constitution is to be considered, in court, as a paramount law." Central to that analysis, it seems to me, is the perception that the Constitution, though it has an effect superior to other laws, is in its nature the sort of "law" that is the business of the courts—an enactment that has a fixed meaning ascertainable through the usual devices familiar to those learned in the law. If the Constitution were not that sort of a "law," but a novel invitation to apply current societal values, what reason would there be to believe that the invitation was addressed to the courts rather than to the legislature? One simply cannot say, regarding that sort of novel enactment, that "[i]t is emphatically the province and duty of the judicial department" to determine its content. Quite to the contrary, the legislature would seem a much more appropriate expositor of social values, and its determination that a statute is compatible with the Constitution should, as in England, prevail.

There is a plausible argument here: If we want the law to reflect social values, the legislature might be the more appropriate institution to do that. In other words, the task of ensuring that law reflects emerging values, or good values, might be one for the elected branches, not for judges. I do not believe that that is quite right, for reasons that we will encounter in chapters 4 and 5. Still, it is a point with which Scalia's critics must engage.

But Scalia's principal argument is different. It is one of "legitimacy," and that argument begs all the important questions.

In brief: Scalia asserts that if courts are to strike down legislation, the only legitimate reason is that the founding document "has a fixed meaning ascertainable through the usual devices familiar to those learned in the law." Really? A fixed meaning of an old law is hardly *sufficient* for legitimacy: Why on earth is it "legitimate," here and now, for judges to strike down laws on the basis of the original public meaning of a document ratified by long-dead people in 1788, and by a small subset of the population no less—one that included no women and not many Black people? How can that be self-evidently legitimate?

Nor is a fixed meaning of an old law *necessary* for legitimacy: *Brown v. Board of Education*, striking down racial segregation, was legitimate, even if it did not speak for the original meaning. If the Supreme Court protects the conditions for self-government, it is not acting illegitimately, even if its rulings do not follow from the original public meaning of a document ratified by dead people centuries ago. The concept of legitimacy raises many puzzles, and in my view, it has caused a lot of confusion in constitutional theory. In this context, it is almost guaranteed to produce circularity. It cannot plausibly be invoked as a ground for public meaning originalism.

By contrast, arguments about what would make our constitutional order better rather than worse have the virtue of mapping out the territory on which the argument about constitutional interpretation should occur. Many originalists focus on the goal of democratic self-government, and they argue that if judges respect the original meaning, they will promote that goal. Recall that one of their goals is to avoid rule by unelected judges. (Good goal!) Perhaps the Constitution, understood in terms of the original public meaning, establishes a well-functioning democratic order. Perhaps its establishment by We the People gives it a kind of pedigree (but recall the fact that the relevant

People are long dead, did not include women, and excluded most Black people).

Perhaps judges, unconstrained by the original public meaning, would make the system less democratic—in part because their substantive judgments would misfire, in part because they are unelected. Perhaps a fixed understanding of the Constitution, promoting stability, will fit with the rule of law, and perhaps alternatives will not, especially if we associate the rule of law with the values of certainty, predictability, and publicity. Consider this illuminating suggestion by Randy Barnett: "Given a sufficiently good constitutional text, originalists maintain that better results will be reached overall if government officials—including judges—must stick to the original meaning rather than empowering them to trump that meaning with one that they prefer."[11] This is an explicit argument that the case for originalism depends on what will produce "better results" overall.[12] As we will see in chapter 4, that case is unconvincing, but Barnett deserves credit here for identifying the territory on which reasonable argument can occur.

It is unfortunate that, like many originalists, Barnett does not give this argument pride of place. His superb book with Evan Bernick, elaborating the original meaning of the Fourteenth Amendment, urges that "we do not start with normative priors," and that "we need an interpretive method in which we are

---

11. See Cass Sunstein and Randy Barnett, "Constitution in Exile?" (2005), available at http://legalaffairs.org/webexclusive/debateclub_cie0505.msp.

12. See also Gary Lawson, On Reading Recipes . . . and Constitutions, *Geo L. J.* 85 (1997): 1823, 1836: "It is highly improbable that any plausible argument for the Constitution's authority can be made that does not, at least to some extent, depend on the Constitution's substance."

confident to identify the law."[13] What matters, in his view, are "theoretical arguments in favor of originalism, not whether originalism produces outcomes that fit one's normative priors." A great deal depends, of course, on what we mean by "theoretical arguments." What are they? As Barnett and Bernick understand the phrase, they are (I think) arguments that stand prior to, and well above, arguments about what would make our system best. If you thought that the idea of interpretation called for originalism, you might have what Barnett and Bernick take to be a theoretical argument on its behalf. If you thought that the idea of legitimacy called for originalism, you might have to be an originalist. If you thought that the very idea of a constitutional order called for originalism, then you would certainly be an originalist.

The problem is that the "theoretical arguments" in favor of originalism are not convincing (see chapter 4); at the very least, they do not establish that originalist approaches are mandatory. In some sense, originalism does indeed stand or fall on whether it "produces outcomes that fit one's normative priors," recognizing that one's priors might be revised, and that "outcomes" include not just particular results in particular cases but also general allocations of authority and consequences for abstract values (the rule of law, self-government, liberty). Originalism is one way "to identify the law," but it is not the only way. To choose among the candidates, everything depends on what would produce "better results" overall. That is the only real question.

In my view, Barnett is right to emphasize the importance of a "sufficiently good constitutional text," understood in light

13. Randy Barnett and Evan Bernick, *The Original Meaning of the Fourteenth Amendment* (2021), 380.

of the original meaning. If the text, understood in light of that meaning, would be horrible, why should we be originalists? It is one thing if the constitutional text, taken only as such, is good, or good enough. It is quite another if it is pretty terrible when understood in light of its original meaning. Imagine, for example, that it is hopelessly undemocratic or that it authorizes or entrenches racial injustice. If so, the argument for sticking with the original meaning would be weakened and collapse. In fact, this is not so far from a plausible account of the American Constitution. The text itself contains broadly appealing phrases, protecting "the freedom of speech" and guaranteeing "due process of law" and "the equal protection of the laws," and vesting executive power in "a president of the United States." If these words were construed in accordance with their original public meaning, our constitutional order would, in my view, be far worse than it is today. (We will get to that.)

I agree that judges should be faithful to the text itself, even if the text were not as good as it is (and it is very good indeed). If judges were not faithful to the text, it is fair to say that they would not be engaged in interpretation at all. In that sense, the idea of interpretation does impose constraints on what judges may do. Moreover, legal systems do much better—and even count as legal systems—if judges are faithful to authoritative texts. If they do not, the rule of law is itself in jeopardy,[14] because judges would appear to be empowered to do whatever they want. In that sense, there is an excellent argument in favor of taking constitutional texts as binding.[15]

---

14. For the best discussion, see Joseph Raz, The Rule of Law and Its Virtue, in *The Authority of Law: Essays on Law and Morality* (1979).

15. Regrettably, this conclusion needs to be qualified. (1) There are historical and normative questions about whether the text is exclusive. Jonathan Gienapp, *The*

Many originalists confuse fidelity to the text with fidelity to the original meaning of the text; *these are not the same thing*. They write as if those who do not believe in following the original meaning do not believe in following the words of the Constitution, or are willing to disregard the Constitution. That is a terrible mistake. And if the consequences of sticking with the original meaning would be terrible, and if those consequences could be avoided with another approach, shouldn't judges consider that other approach?

These questions are not (quite) meant to be rhetorical; they suggest only that various approaches to interpretation are on the table. As we have seen, many originalists find it both appropriate and necessary to argue that the consequences of their approach would not be terrible. With Barnett, they urge that those consequences would be good or even great. They contend that their approach fits with a great deal of existing constitutional doctrine, or at least with those aspects of it that seem least dispensable. Few contemporary originalists are willing to concede that under their approach, racial segregation is constitutionally acceptable—even though nothing in the original meaning bans segregation by the national government, and even though it is not at all easy to show that the Constitution bans segregation at the state level. Contemporary originalists do not often acknowledge that their approach would allow the national government to prohibit women from working for the federal civil service, or would freely allow states to discriminate against women—even though those are, in all likelihood, necessary implications of most forms of originalism.

Second Creation (2018). (2) In a few cases, the Court has not followed the text, and that is widely regarded as acceptable. See David A. Strauss, *The Living Constitution* (2010).

It is noteworthy that originalists tend either to say little about the difficulty of squaring their approach with foundational commitments of the contemporary constitutional order, or to insist that the difficulty is not so severe, because originalism already embodies those commitments. Some originalists work extremely hard to try to demonstrate that point.[16] They are right to do so, because the argument for their approach depends on that work (as we shall see in more detail in chapter 4). Whether or not that argument is convincing, it is noteworthy that some of those who stress original meaning find it necessary to stress these points about the acceptable or admirable consequences of their preferred approach. They do not rest content with, or even make, the claim that their approach is built into the very idea of interpretation. The same is true for those who invoke claims about moral or political legitimacy.

Indeed, some originalists, notably Jack Balkin, embrace semantic originalism and emphasize that certain provisions of the Constitution are written in general and abstract terms, which allow accommodation of evolving understandings.[17] Some people who hold this view contend that the original understanding was that the Constitution creates broad principles whose concrete meaning would not be frozen in time.[18] If their claim is about the intended meaning, or about the original public meaning, it is not clear that they are right as a matter of history; the evidence is ambiguous here. But if they are, the line between originalism and other approaches starts to dissolve,

16. Barnett and Bernick, *The Original Meaning of the Fourteenth Amendment*.

17. See Jack Balkin, *Living Originalism* (2012).

18. See H. Jefferson Powell, *The Original Understanding of Original Intent*, *Har. L. Rev.* 98 (1985): 885.

because interpretation of abstractions—what counts as "equal protection" or "the freedom of speech"—squarely invites the exercise of discretion on the part of the judges. And if Balkin's approach to interpretation is correct, my main conclusion holds: It is not because of anything intrinsic to the idea of interpretation, but because adoption of his approach would make our constitutional system better rather than worse.

What Our Law Is

In chapter 1, we encountered the claim that our legal system simply *is* originalist. Let us step back and note that in making that claim, Baude and Sachs offer an independent objection to my central argument here, and that objection needs to be discussed independently.

Baude and Sachs urge that we need to distinguish between two kinds of theories of constitutional interpretation: (1) theories that reflect what our law is (that is, theories that reflect what judges have long done or thought) and (2) theories that call for some kind of change or reform (that is, theories that would abandon what judges have long done or thought).[19] Suppose that the American legal system actually were originalist or Thayerian, in the sense that American judges just applied originalism or Thayerism, and did so consistently (from, say, 1800). If so, an argument for moral readings would be an effort to uproot our system. Perhaps that argument could be made convincing on the ground that it would make our constitutional system better rather than worse. But it would have to acknowledge that it is

19. See William Baude and Stephen E. Sachs, Grounding Originalism, *Nw.U. L. Rev.* 113 (2019).

not, in fact, consistent with our long-standing law, which was, by hypothesis, originalist or Thayerian (from 1800).

In my view, Baude and Sachs are right to draw attention to the law of interpretation, understood as the legal rules that judges have endorsed about how to interpret the Constitution. But I do not think that they are right in arguing that our system is originalist. In my view, it is hard indeed to see how that argument can find support in actual practice. Consider just a few examples of decisions that are very hard to square with the original public meaning of the founding document:

- *Bolling v. Sharpe* (1954), striking down racial segregation by the national government;[20]
- *New York Times v. Sullivan* (1964), understanding the First Amendment to impose serious restrictions on the use of state libel law;[21]
- *Brandenburg v. Ohio* (1969), offering broad protection to speech under a version of the "clear and present danger" test;[22]
- *Police Department of Chicago v. Mosley* (1972), suggesting a strong presumption against content discrimination under the First Amendment;[23]
- *Califano v. Goldfarb* (1977), striking down sex discrimination by the national government;[24]
- *Lujan v. Defenders of Wildlife* (1992), striking down congressional efforts to allow "citizen suits";[25]

20. 357 U.S. 497 (1954).
21. 376 U.S. 254 (1964).
22. 395 U.S. 444 (1969).
23. 408 U.S. 92 (1972).
24. 430 U.S. 199 (1977).
25. 504 U.S. 555 (1992).

- *Lucas v. South Carolina Coast Council* (1992), understanding the Fifth and Fourteenth Amendments to protect against "regulatory takings";[26]
- *Lawrence v. Texas* (2003), striking down bans on same-sex sodomy.[27]

The sheer number of cases that seem wildly inconsistent with the original public meaning makes it exceedingly difficult to argue that originalism is "our law." And the problem is compounded by the many cases that might, either plausibly or through fancy footwork, be squared with originalism *but that were not originally written in originalist terms.* The above catalog starts from cases in the 1950s, which means that it reflects well over sixty years of practice. And while this is not the place to do that, I believe that we could find countless cases starting in the 1790s that are not originalist, which means that we are dealing with well over two hundred years of practice.

Baude and Sachs are both careful and inventive, and they are entirely aware that much of current constitutional law is not consistent with originalism. They might well say that despite all those cases, many judges would be greatly troubled if it could be demonstrated that a past ruling, or a proposed ruling, would be clearly inconsistent with the original meaning. But what should we do with that fact? Countless rulings did not rest, or purport to rest, on the original meaning. Countless rulings did not claim support in the original meaning. Countless rulings did not even refer to the original meaning! How, then, can originalism possibly be our law?

26. 505 U.S. 1003 (1992).
27. 539 U.S. 558 (2003).

Over the last one hundred years, our law has been some combination of textualism, democracy reinforcement, moral readings, common-law constitutionalism, and common-good constitutionalism, whatever time period we choose. Originalism certainly makes appearances in Supreme Court opinions. But it is emphatically not our law.

Fit and Justification

Let us now shift to nonoriginalist approaches. Are they legitimate forms of interpretation? (To get slightly ahead of the story: Yes, no doubt about it.) Are they in some sense compulsory? (To get slightly ahead of the story: Absolutely not.) How then can we decide whether to accept them? (That is for chapter 4. No peeking.)

Suppose a judge thinks, with Ely, that where the Constitution is vague or open-textured, she should interpret it to make the democratic process work as well as it possibly can. Is that approach ruled off-limits by the very idea of interpretation? It is hard to see why it would be. As noted, Justice Breyer has argued that a democracy-protective approach to freedom of speech, honoring "active liberty," fits with the text and purposes of the document even if that approach produces results that are not compelled by or consistent with the original meaning, narrowly conceived. (Recall that some originalists think that the Constitution was deliberately written in broad terms whose meaning was meant to evolve over time.) Breyer's approach must be evaluated on its merits; it cannot be ruled off the table. Breyer is candid about this point, and contends that the consequences of his preferred approach would be good.

The same can be said for Dworkin's preferred view, to the effect that the Constitution should be taken to include abstractions that invite moral reasoning from judges, and that judges must give those generalities the best moral readings that they can. Indeed, both the *Lochner* Court in the early decades of the twentieth century,[28] which struck down minimum wage and maximum hour legislation, and the Warren Court,[29] which did a host of things approved by progressives in the 1950s and 1960s, approached the Constitution in this way. Many people, on both the right and the left, think the Court should resume something like this approach today.[30] They want a lot of moral readings, perhaps to forbid abortion, perhaps to protect a right to health care. Whether or not they are the right approach, moral readings would certainly count as interpretation within permissible understandings of the term.

As an advocate of moral readings, Dworkin argued that legal interpretation involves two obligations.[31] The first obligation is one of "fit"; an interpreter cannot simply ignore the materials that are being interpreted. The second is one of "justification." What Dworkin meant is that within the constraints of fit, an interpreter must justify the existing legal materials in the sense of making them the best that they can be. To explain this approach, Dworkin offered the arresting analogy of a chain novel. Suppose that you are the fifth writer in a chain, and that your task is to write the fifth chapter. Four writers have written four chapters before you. In writing the fifth chapter, you must write the novel that others have started, and not another. You cannot make up a whole new novel. If it looks like a romance, you had

28. See Lochner v. New York, 198 U.S. 45 (1905).

29. See, e.g., Brown v. Board of Education, 347 U.S. 483 (1954); Reynolds v. Simms, 377 U.S. 533 (1964).

30. Richard A. Epstein, *The Classical Constitution* (2014), seems to me in this vein.

31. Ronald Dworkin, *Law's Empire* (1985).

better not turn it into horror. Nor can you depart from what has come before, in the sense of producing a narrative that ignores it or makes it unintelligible or random or gibberish. But you might well think that you have an obligation to make the novel good rather than terrible, perhaps the best it can possibly be, and your authorship of the next chapter will be undertaken with that obligation in mind.

Dworkin was right to observe that at least in American constitutional law, judicial judgments often seem a lot like that. (In fact, we could apply the idea of a chain novel well beyond American law and well beyond constitutional law.) It is generally agreed that in the American constitutional system, judges who interpret the Constitution owe a duty of fidelity to what has come before (acknowledging that egregiously erroneous rulings can be overruled). But judges also have a lot of discretion. They can turn the tale in one direction or another. If, for example, the question is whether the Constitution requires states to recognize same-sex marriage, or allows the government to punish certain lies online, they must ask: What approach makes the best sense out of the existing materials? If the Court has ruled that the Constitution does not protect the right to choose abortion, they must ask: What about the right not to be sterilized?

An emphasis on fit and justification leaves many questions open. A recurring question is the relationship among the decided cases, long-standing social traditions, and the original public meaning of the text. What does the obligation of fit mean when these point in different directions? Different answers to that question are admissible within the general concept of interpretation. Justice Clarence Thomas favors the original public meaning, and he would give it priority over the decided cases. Justice Antonin Scalia also liked the original public meaning, but on important occasions he would defer to the precedents, even if they violated the original understanding. As he once said to a group of faculty at the University of Chicago Law School, "I am an originalist, but I'm not crazy!"

If you believe in moral readings, you might respect precedent even if it defies your view about the best moral reading. Or maybe not. In *Brown v. Board of Education*, the Supreme Court seemed pretty comfortable rejecting its long-standing precedent allowing racial segregation; and in *Lawrence v. Texas*, upholding the right to engage in same-sex sexual relations and overruling its prior rulings to the contrary, the Court said this:[32]

> The present case does not involve minors. It does not involve persons who might be injured or coerced or who are situated in relationships where consent might not easily be refused. It does not involve public conduct or prostitution. It does not involve whether the government must give formal recognition to any relationship that homosexual persons seek to enter. The case does involve two adults who, with full and mutual consent from each other, engaged in sexual practices common to a homosexual lifestyle. The petitioners are entitled to respect for their private lives. The State cannot demean their existence or control their destiny by making their private sexual conduct a crime. Their right to liberty under the Due Process Clause gives them the full right to engage in their conduct without intervention of the government.

This, then, is a moral reading that embodies a willingness to reject precedent.

On the basis of Dworkin's argument, we might be tempted to think (as Dworkin does) that there is one thing that legal

32. Lawrence v. Texas, 539 U.S. 558, 578 (2003).

interpretation just is: an attempt to ensure both fit and justification. And it is true that originalists and moral readers, Thayerians and democracy reinforcers, common-law constitutionalists
and common-good constitutionalists—all of these, and more,
might be willing to embrace the view that both fit and justification matter. But the temptation should be resisted. While
Dworkin's approach is one conception of interpretation, it is
not the only one.

If we believe that interpretation involves the search for authorial intentions, we will not much care about fit and justification. We will attempt to identify a *fact*: What did the relevant
author(s) intend? It is true that the answer to that question
might be difficult to find, and it is also true that there may be no
answer to that question. But if so, we may have exhausted the
act of interpretation. Something similar can be said about those
who emphasize the original public meaning. They want to adhere to it; they do not focus on fit and justification. Theirs is one
view (again, not the only one) of what interpretation is.

I have gone into a fair bit of detail here, but let us not lose the
main thread. Reasonable people can and do understand interpretation in different ways. Radically different approaches can
fairly count as interpretive. Which approach is best? How
can we answer that question? We will get to that in chapter 4.

Interpretation and Construction

To fill out the picture, we need to shift one more time. Some
people, including some prominent originalists, have insisted on
the crucial importance of making a distinction between "interpretation" and "construction."[33] On one view, interpreters have

33. See Keith Whittington, *Constitutional Construction* (1999).

to, or should, follow the original public meaning. But sometimes there really isn't an original public meaning, or at least there isn't one that can answer a specific question. Consider, as a possible example, the question of whether and to what extent the First Amendment protects spending on political campaigns. As Gertrude Stein said about Oakland, "There is no there there." Originalists agree that on important occasions, there is no there there. What then? A possible answer is "construction."

In a clear and illuminating discussion, Lawrence Solum suggests that interpretation attempts to discover the *linguistic meaning* of a legal text, whereas construction gives *legal effect* to that meaning.[34] (Solum understands the linguistic meaning to go beyond the semantic meaning and to include the original public meaning.) The First Amendment, for example, has a linguistic meaning; the "freedom of speech" does not refer to bowling or skating. At the same time, it is not easy to argue that the linguistic meaning requires various First Amendment doctrines: the exclusion of obscenity, the reduced level of protection given to commercial advertising, the distinction between content-based restrictions on speech ("no one may criticize the president") and content-neutral restrictions ("no one may advertise on subways"). As a public meaning originalist, Solum urges that interpretation "is guided by linguistic facts— facts about patterns of usage,"[35] and is value-free or only "thinly normative,"[36] in the sense that our normative views about what

---

34. See Lawrence Solum, The Interpretation-Construction Distinction, *Constitutional Commentary* 27 (2010): 95. As Solum emphasizes, the distinction has a long history and has been understood in several different ways.

35. Solum, The Interpretation-Construction Distinction, 104.

36. Solum, 104.

the law should be are not the source of our judgments about whether an interpretation is correct.

By contrast, "theories of construction are ultimately normative," in the sense that a judgment on behalf of one construction rather than another turns on "premises that go beyond linguistic facts."[37] In Solum's terminology, a Thayerian approach that favors deference to the political process is a theory of construction; it is unquestionably normative, even if it does not allow judges to enlist their own moral or political beliefs in particular cases. When the original public meaning of a text is vague or ambiguous (as it might turn out to be for many constitutional provisions), then the fact that judges are involved in construction, rather than interpretation, seems obvious. On Solum's view, judges may end up in a "construction zone."[38] For judges who find themselves in that zone, there are many ways to proceed; deference to the political process is merely one.

If we accept this distinction, then we might say that there is nothing that *construction* just is (except at a high level of generality), because construction cannot occur without some kind of normative argument, and because several (or many) normative arguments are consistent with the basic idea of construction. But on this view, there is something that *interpretation* just is, which is the elicitation of the original public meaning. We have seen that Solum offers several arguments on behalf of originalism. He argues that "as a matter of fact, the meaning of a given constitutional provision is fixed at the time of origin by its original public meaning," and also that "as a matter of fact, the semantic content makes some contribution to American law." In his view, "these factual claims are not based on

37. Solum, 104.
38. Solum, 104.

arguments of political morality" but instead rest on an understanding of how "communication through language works."[39]
Solum seeks to "derive conclusions about constitutional meaning
from nonnormative premises—that is, on the basis of premises
that are not ethic or moral in nature."[40] On this account, there is
something that interpretation just is, and it is originalism. (As we
have seen, Solum also argues that originalism leads to a better
system of constitutional law.) Solum's defense of this position
is careful and complex. But in the end, an understanding of
"how communication through language works" cannot possibly justify use of the original public meaning.

   To defend his conclusion, Solum enlists an analogy: If we
read a letter from centuries ago, and if it contains (for example)
the word "awful," we will interpret it by asking about the meaning of that word when the letter was written (awe-inspiring, as
was often the valence then), not by consulting modern dictionaries. That is true. If we consult modern dictionaries, we will
have no idea what the letter meant. And in constitutional law,
we might be willing to accept semantic originalism; that is what
the analogy might suggest. But the analogy is not sufficient to
support use of the original public meaning. The Constitution is
not an old letter, and whether we should interpret it as we
would interpret such a letter is the question to be decided. The
analogy does not prove that we should. In fact, the analogy does
not work at all.

   To see why, consider the view that judges should decide, as
a matter of *principle*, whether current practices do deny people

39. Lawrence B. Solum, "Semantic Originalism," Illinois Public Law Research
Paper no. 07-24 (2008), 8, available at http://papers.ssrn.com/sol3/papers.cfm
?abstract_id=1120244.
   40. Solum, "Semantic Originalism," 10.

"equal protection of the laws," or violate "the freedom of speech," rather than ask about the original meaning of those words. Whether that view is right or wrong is a normative question. It cannot be settled by an understanding of how communication through language works. Philosophical work on that topic does not resolve the question of the appropriate judicial role undertaken under the capacious rubric of "interpretation."

Possible Worlds

No approach to constitutional interpretation makes sense in every imaginable nation or in every possible world. The argument for any particular approach must depend, in large part, on a set of judgments about which institutions we can trust most, and for what, and which institutions we can trust least, and for what—above all, about the strengths and weaknesses of legislatures and courts. If judges are excellent and error-free, their excellence and freedom from error bear on the choice of a theory of interpretation. If judges are terrible and likely to blunder, their terribleness bears on the choice of a theory of interpretation.

Return to Thayerism: Courts should uphold legislation unless it is plainly and unambiguously in violation of the Constitution. Because the Constitution is frequently ambiguous, Thayer's approach would require courts to uphold almost all legislation—including school segregation in the District of Columbia, sex discrimination in federal employment, affirmative action, restrictions on abortion, mandatory school prayer, restrictions on free speech, and much more. In these circumstances, it should be unsurprising that most judges assert their right to interpret the Constitution independently and refuse to accept the legislature's view merely because the document is

THE INEVITABILITY OF CHOICE 89

ambiguous. In the last half-century, no member of the Court has been willing to endorse the proposition that legislation should be upheld unless the founding document clearly forbids it.

But imagine a society in which democratic processes work exceedingly fairly and well, so that judicial intervention is almost never required from the standpoint of anything that really matters.[41] In such a society, racial segregation does not occur. Political processes are fair, and political speech is never banned. The legitimate claims of religious minorities and property holders are respected. The systems of federalism and separation of powers are safeguarded, and precisely to the right extent, by democratic institutions.

Imagine, too, that in this society, the judgments of judges are highly unreliable. From the standpoint of political morality, judges make systematic blunders when they attempt to give content to constitutional terms such as "equal protection of the laws" and "due process of law." Resolving constitutional questions without respecting the views of the legislature, courts would make society much worse, because their understandings of rights and institutions are so bad. In such a society, a Thayerian approach to the Constitution would make a great deal of

---

41. See Jeremy Waldron, The Core of the Case against Judicial Review, Yale L. Rev. 115 (2006): 1346, 1360: "We are to imagine a society with (1) democratic institutions in reasonably good working order, including a representative legislature elected on the basis of universal adult suffrage; (2) a set of judicial institutions, again in reasonably good order, set up on a nonrepresentative basis to hear individual lawsuits, settle disputes, and uphold the rule of law; (3) a commitment on the part of most members of the society and most of its officials to the idea of individual and minority rights; and (4) persisting, substantial, and good faith disagreement about rights (i.e., about what the commitment to rights actually amounts to and what its implications are) among the members of the society who are committed to the idea of rights."

sense, and judges should be persuaded to adopt it. These are extreme assumptions, of course, but even if they are softened significantly, the argument for a Thayerian approach might be convincing, all things considered.

Or consider a society in which democratic processes work poorly, in the sense that they do not live up to democratic ideals, and also in which political majorities invade fundamental rights—say, freedom of religion and freedom of speech. Suppose that in this society, judges are trustworthy, in the sense that they can make democratic processes work better (say, by safeguarding the right to vote), and also that they can protect fundamental rights, as they really should be understood. In such a society, the argument for democracy reinforcement, and for moral readings, would be quite strong.

Now turn to moral readings. Many people reject the idea that judges should give them; they think that moral readings are too unmoored or dangerous. Who are judges, to tell us what morality requires? Maybe that is a decisive objection.

But imagine a society in which the original public meaning of the Constitution is not so excellent, in the sense that it does not adequately protect rights, properly understood, and in the sense that it calls for institutional arrangements (say, between Congress and the president) that become obsolete over time, as new circumstances and fresh needs arise. Imagine that in this society, the democratic process is pretty good but far from great, in the sense that it sometimes produces or permits significant injustices. Suppose finally that in this society, judges will do very well if they offer moral readings, built modestly and incrementally on their own precedents. In such a society, moral readings of the Constitution would have a great deal of appeal.

We should now be able to see that none of these approaches is ruled out by the Constitution itself. Each can be implemented in a way that firmly respects the document's text and attempts to interpret it. The question is how to do so. If the founding document set out the rules for its own interpretation, judges would be bound by those rules (though any such rules would themselves need to be interpreted). But the Constitution sets out no such rules. For this reason, any approach to the document must be defended by reference to some account that is supplied by the interpreter (with due respect for existing law).

The meaning of the Constitution must be made rather than found, not in the grand (and preposterous) sense that it is entirely up for grabs, but in the more mundane sense that it must be settled by an account of interpretation that it does not itself contain. The idea of interpretation is capacious, and a range of approaches fit within it. Among the reasonable alternatives, any particular approach to the Constitution must be defended on the ground that it makes the relevant constitutional order better rather than worse.

3

The Oath of Office

ARTICLE VI of the Constitution says this:

> This Constitution, and the laws of the United States which shall be made in pursuance thereof; and all treaties made, or which shall be made, under the authority of the United States, shall be the supreme law of the land; and the judges in every state shall be bound thereby, anything in the Constitution or laws of any State to the contrary notwithstanding.
>
> The Senators and Representatives before mentioned, and the members of the several state legislatures, and all executive and judicial officers, both of the United States and of the several states, shall be bound by oath or affirmation, to support this Constitution; but no religious test shall ever be required as a qualification to any office or public trust under the United States.`

The "supreme law of the land" includes "This Constitution," and federal officers (along with state legislators) are "bound, by oath or affirmation, to support this Constitution." Do these words have implications for constitutional interpretation? Might they settle long-standing debates?

Some people think so.[1] Emphasizing the importance of the oath, Christopher Green concludes: "Those who swear the Article VI oath should . . . take the historic textually expressed sense as interpretively paramount."[2] On one view, the term "this Constitution" is equivalent to "the original public meaning of this Constitution,"[3] and perhaps the oath requires that conclusion. This view is worth engaging, because it has received a lot of attention; some originalists have invoked the oath to support originalism. In their view, the oath seals the deal in their favor. If you take the oath, you simply have to be an originalist.

That is quite wrong. What is wrong with it tells us a lot about what kind of freedom judges (and others) have in constitutional interpretation.

1. See Christopher Green, "This Constitution": Constitutional Indexicals as a Basis for Textualist Semi-Originalism, *No.D. L. Rev.* 84 (2009): 1607, for a clear treatment. Green does not rely solely on the phrase "this Constitution"; he emphasizes several temporal indexicals (see 1657–66). See also Evan Bernick and Christopher Green, "What Is the Object of the Constitutional Oath?" (2020), available at https://papers.ssrn.com/sol3/papers.cfm?abstract_id=3441234; William Pryor, Against Living Common-Goodism, *Federalist Society Review* 23 (2022): 25.

2. Green, "'This Constitution,'" 1674.

3. See Pryor, "Against Living Common-Goodism." For discussion, see Christopher R. Green, Originalism and the Sense–Reference Distinction, *St.Lo. L. J.* 50 (2006); Green, "'This Constitution'"; Cass R. Sunstein, Originalism, *No.D. L. Rev.* 93 (2018): 1671. For valuable and exceptionally illuminating general accounts, see Richard H. Fallon Jr., The Chimerical Concept of Original Public Meaning, *Va. L. Rev.* 107 (2021): 1421; Lawrence B. Solum, The Public Meaning Thesis: An Originalist Account of Constitutional Meaning, *B.U. L. Rev.* 101, no. 1953 (2021); Solum, Originalism versus Living Constitutionalism, *Nw.U. L. Rev.* 113 (2019): 1243; Solum, The Fixation Thesis: The Role of Historical Fact in Original Meaning, *No.D. L. Rev.* 91, no. 1 (2015); Solum, "The Constraint Principle: Original Meaning and Constitutional Practice" (March 24, 2017) (unpublished manuscript), https://papers.ssrn.com/sol3/papers.cfm?abstract_id=2940215.

Let us begin with the text. Simply as a matter of language, the referent of "this Constitution" is not at all unclear.[4] It is the written Constitution of which Article VI is a part. The word "this" is what philosophers and linguists call an "indexical." Words like "now," "here," and "this" direct us to their referent. It follows that the word "this" in the phrase "this Constitution" points to the written text of the Constitution of the United States, in which the phrase appears. Other constitutions—the German, Danish, Irish, and Austrian constitutions, for example—are not part of "the supreme law of the land." Public officials are not bound, by oath or affirmation, to support other constitutions. They are bound to support "this" Constitution. That much is straightforward.

For orientation, now turn to some questions.

1. Does the First Amendment protect libelous speech?[5]
2. Does the Equal Protection Clause or the Privileges or Immunities Clause forbid racial segregation?[6]
3. Does the Equal Protection Clause or the Privileges or Immunities Clause forbid sex discrimination?[7]

---

4. See Green, "'This Constitution,'" 1649–53. Alas (from the standpoint of conceptual clarity), some serious qualifications come from Jonathan Gienapp, *The Second Creation* (2018). Gienapp emphasizes that it was not at all clear, immediately after ratification, what the Constitution was, exactly, and what its relationship was to what preceded it. The rise of a consensus in favor of the idea of a fixed written constitution may well have come in the decade *after* ratification. Among other things, Gienapp urges that the Constitution was "a 'first draught' . . . a work in progress, in need of activation and subsequent work—in essence an imperfect and unfinished object" (81).

5. See New York Times v. Sullivan, 376 U.S. 254 (1964).

6. See Brown v. Board of Education, 347 U.S. 483 (1954).

7. See Craig v. Boren, 428 U.S. 190 (1976).

4. Does the vesting of legislative power in Congress forbid Congress from granting broad discretion to administrative agencies?[8]

5. Does the vesting of executive power in a president of the United States forbid Congress from creating independent regulatory agencies?[9]

6. Does the Takings Clause forbid regulatory takings, or is it limited to physical takings?[10]

7. Does Article III of the Constitution require plaintiffs to show an "injury in fact"?[11]

8. Does the Fourteenth Amendment forbid affirmative action programs?[12]

9. Does the Fifth or Fourteenth Amendment forbid racial discrimination by Congress?[13]

Now ask: How may, or how must, those who take the oath of office approach such questions?

Suppose that we accept semantic originalism and understand originalism to entail it, and to entail nothing more. If so, there is a strong argument that oath-takers are indeed bound by the original *semantic* meaning of the Constitution. To be president, someone must be at least thirty-five years of age; the impeachment power is not vested in the federal judiciary; there is a right to trial by jury, not to trial by magistrate. If the semantic meaning of words shifts over time, it is fair to say that what is binding is the original semantic meaning, not some new

---

8. See Gundy v. U.S., 588 U.S. (2019).

9. See Humphrey's Executor v. U.S., 295 U.S. 602 (1935).

10. See Lucas v. South Carolina Coast Council, 505 U.S. 1003 (1992).

11. See Lujan v. Defenders of Wildlife, 504 U.S. 555 (1992).

12. See Regents of the University of California v. Bakke, 438 U.S. 265 (1978).

13. See Bolling v. Sharpe, 347 U.S. 497 (1954).

semantic meaning. Almost everyone almost always accepts semantic originalism.[14] As we have seen, the challenge is that purely semantic originalism leaves constitutional meaning wide open, at least on contested issues. It probably does not answer *any* of the questions posed above; it is hard, in practice, to see it as forbidding any reasonable form of "living constitutionalism." Those who believe that they reject originalism are entirely comfortable with semantic originalism.

Does the oath require use of the original intentions or original public meaning? The answer to that question is no.

Around the world, many constitutions use a phrase of this kind ("this Constitution"), and yet it is generally understood that they should *not* be interpreted in terms of either form of originalism, or in terms that make originalism a distinctive approach to constitutional interpretation.[15] This fact strongly suggests that the phrase "this Constitution" need not be taken to entail any particular view about how to interpret it, and that those who take an oath to support it need not endorse any reasonable theory of interpretation, though they might well have to choose one. To see the point, note that we could imagine a constitution that uses the phrase "this constitution" that was also thought and understood—before, during, or after ratification—to include a set of general concepts (say, "the freedom of speech" or "executive power") whose meaning in particular cases would change over time. In other words, we could

14. We need the term "almost" in view of some well-known puzzles for semantic originalism, including the application of equal protection principles to the federal government. See Bolling v. Sharpe, 347 U.S. 497 (1954). Did the justices who signed *Bolling v. Sharpe* violate their oath of office? That would be a strong claim.

15. See Conor Casey and Adrian Vermeule, Argument by Slogan, *Harvard Journal of Law and Public Policy: Per Curiam* (2022), available at https://www.harvard-jlpp .com/argument-by-slogan-conor-casey-and-adrian-vermeule/.

imagine a constitution that was understood, as a matter of historical fact by those who ratified it, to call for semantic originalism (but nothing else). If so, public meaning originalism would not support public meaning originalism!

Suppose, however, that as a matter of historical fact, the ratifiers of the U.S. Constitution unanimously understood "this Constitution" in terms that fit with public meaning originalism. Suppose that they thought that they were one and the same, so that any effort to separate them would have been unintelligible. What then? Would the oath require officials to follow the ratifiers? The answer is a firm no, but getting there will be just a little complicated.

We might think that this question immediately raises, or essentially is, another: *the level of generality problem.* Is the phrase "the freedom of speech" to be interpreted in terms of a specific set of understandings (protecting, say, political dissent and commercial advertising, but not blasphemy or obscenity)? Or should it be understood to set out an abstract term, whose specific consequences are not frozen in time, and might even change dramatically over a period of decades?

If we agree that "this Constitution" is "the original public meaning of this Constitution," then perhaps we will also agree, consistent with public meaning originalism, that the proper solution to the level of generality problem must be *historical.* One more time: It is a matter of uncovering a *fact.* If so, whether a constitutional phrase was originally understood to be specific and fixed, or instead abstract and susceptible to different specifications over the time, is not a philosophical or normative question. It is a question about the original public meaning. To be sure, it might be exceedingly difficult to answer that question as a matter of history. But at least we have identified the right question, if we are to be faithful to "this Constitution." Or so it might be concluded.

Now we arrive at the heart of the matter. Whether "this Constitution" should be identified with any particular historical understanding of how to interpret it is not, in fact, a question of history or one of fact.

To see why, suppose that the ratifiers did, in fact, embrace a particular view of interpretation, and that that view just is the original public meaning; suppose too that constitutional terms did have specific public meanings. Without circularity, *we cannot say that the original public meaning is binding because the original public meaning was that the original public meaning is binding.* The same would be true if we substitute the term *original understanding* for *original public meaning.* (I use the two terms interchangeably.) The original public meaning may or may not be the best way to interpret "this Constitution," but it is simply not the same as "this Constitution." Public meaning originalism may or may not be the right approach to interpretation, but it is not required by the oath.

Pointing to both text and history, Professor Green urges:[16]

> "This Constitution" is, then, located at the time of the Founding. The constituting of the United States happened at the Founding. It did not happen over generations and does not happen anew every day. The constitutional author distinguished itself from succeeding generations, identified its work of establishing the Constitution with the Founding's ratifying conventions, and spoke of the Founding as the time of its adoption. If we ask the Constitution what time it is— that is, what it means by the term "now"—it answers with the time of the Founding.

16. Green, "'This Constitution,'" 1666.

In an important sense, these claims are correct. The constituting of the United States did indeed happen at the founding, and if we define that idea in a certain way, that is the only time that it happened. (True, we could define it in other ways, in which case it might happen anew every day.) But does it follow, from these claims, that "this Constitution" must be understood in accordance with its original public meaning? Not at all.

Those who take the oath are and must be bound by "this Constitution," and none other. But they need not agree that the meaning of the Constitution is identical to that which would follow from the original public meaning.

No one should doubt that the "supreme law of the land" includes "This Constitution," and that federal officers are "bound, by oath or affirmation, to support this Constitution." Those of us who were privileged to take the oath do so solemnly swear. But people with different views about constitutional interpretation, and with favorable or unfavorable views about different forms of originalism, can agree to "support this Constitution." Nothing in the oath requires officials to subscribe to a particular conception of interpretation. Diverse judges, and diverse officials, can "support this Constitution" while having diverse views about how to interpret it.

Here is another way to put the point. Throughout American history, many distinguished judges have not been self-identified originalists, and they did not spend a lot of time on the original understanding or the original public meaning. (That is an understatement.)[17] Clear examples include Oliver Wendell

---

17. It might be tempting to note that the term "originalism" is relatively new, and to insist that for that reason, the fact that justices and judges did not embrace it, before it was a term, is not exactly surprising. The point is correct but not responsive. What I am emphasizing is not that the relevant people did not use the term; *they did not practice originalism in any form.* (At least they did not do it that often. In fact, they almost never did.)

Holmes, Louis Brandeis, Felix Frankfurter, Benjamin Cardozo, Charles Evans Hughes, Robert Jackson, John Marshall Harlan II, Thurgood Marshall, Lewis Powell, Ruth Bader Ginsburg, Henry Friendly, Harold Leventhal, Stephen Williams, and Richard Posner. It would be remarkable—a kind of miracle—if all of these justices violated their oath of office, or if they made some fundamental mistake about the meaning of the word "this."

The claim that the term "this Constitution" mandates a contested theory of interpretation belongs in the same category with many other efforts to resolve controversial questions in law by reference to the supposed dictate of some external authority. Whether maddening or liberating, the truth is that in important cases, there is no such dictate. The choice is ours.

4

How to Choose

There are some questions which we feel must be answered in a
certain way.

—JOHN RAWLS

We do not believe that adopting the original meaning of the
Fourteenth Amendment as a whole would lead to *results* that
differ radically from those that current doctrine would
produce. Far from it.

—RANDY BARNETT AND EVAN BERNICK

NOW WE arrive at the heart of the matter.

Suppose that a theory of constitutional interpretation would
lead to the conclusion that the federal government may discriminate on the basis of race; that federal and state governments can ban speech that they consider to be dangerous; that
federal and state governments are free to discriminate on the
basis of sex. Does it count against a theory of interpretation that
it would lead to those results, or would that conclusion be intolerably "result-oriented"? Or suppose that a theory of interpretation would require a long list of outcomes that would be

palpably unjust or even brutal. Is that a problem? Potentially a decisive objection? (Short answer: Yes.)

My main claim in this chapter, and indeed in this book, is that in order to choose a theory of constitutional interpretation, judges (and others) must seek "reflective equilibrium," in which their judgments, at multiple levels of generality, are brought into alignment with one another.[1] Indeed, I will be suggesting that *there is no other way to choose a theory of constitutional interpretation*. It follows that judges (and others) must consider the consequences of their choice for particular judgments that operate, for them, as provisional "fixed points," understood as judgments that seem both clear and firm. If a theory of interpretation would allow the federal government to discriminate on the basis of race and sex, it is unlikely to be a good theory of interpretation; it is at least presumptively unacceptable for that reason.

I have used the term "provisional fixed points," and in this respect I am following John Rawls, who emphasizes both their importance and their provisional character in moral and political philosophy. A judge might believe something with real conviction. Even so, a judge ought to be willing to listen to counterarguments; humility is a good thing. Few points are so fixed that nothing at all could dislodge them. Still, people have beliefs

---

1. My colleague Richard Fallon has explored the idea of reflective equilibrium, and its relationship to constitutional law, to superb effect in his *Law and Legitimacy in the Supreme Court* (2018). I arrived there independently, but he was there first, and I have learned a great deal from his work, with which I am in broad agreement. The idea of reflective equilibrium is also used to good effect in Lawrence Solum, Themes from Fallon on Constitutional Theory, *Georgetown Journal of Law and Public Policy* 18 (2020): 287; Mitchell N. Berman, Reflective Equilibrium and Constitutional Method: Lessons from John McCain and the Natural-Born Citizenship Clause, *Faculty Scholarship at Penn Carey Law* (2011): 2349.

about constitutional meaning that it would be exceptionally difficult, at least, to dislodge. They are likely to have an assortment of such beliefs. What I am urging here is that that is entirely fine. Fixed points about particular cases are central to assessments of theories of constitutional interpretation.

You might respond that the choice of a theory of interpretation cannot possibly depend on the results that it yields. You might think that that choice has to be made on the basis of some commitment that might seem higher or more fundamental. If we focus on results, and choose a theory of interpretation on the basis of results, perhaps we are biased, or unforgivably "result-oriented," and engaged in some kind of special pleading.

The problem with that response (I shall be suggesting) is that it rests on an illusion of compulsion. We have seen that among the reasonable candidates, judges (and others) are not compelled to adopt a particular theory of interpretation; they must make a choice. One more time: To do that, judges (and others) are required to think about what would make our constitutional order better rather than worse. As we will see, and as I will be emphasizing, we should not consider, as fixed points, only results about particular cases (though they matter a lot). We must also consider defining ideals (including self-government and the rule of law), and we must think about processes and institutions. There might be fixed points there as well.

These claims are meant, of course, to insist on the connection between the search for reflective equilibrium and foundational questions about constitutional law. In *A Theory of Justice*, John Rawls elaborates the basic idea for purposes of moral and political philosophy.[2] He begins with this suggestion: "There are

2. See John Rawls, *A Theory of Justice* (1971), 18.

some questions which we feel must be answered in a certain way. For example, we are confident that religious intolerance and racial discrimination are unjust."[3] (Who is the "we," you might ask? A fair and important question, to which I will return.) On some issues, we are confident that we "have reached what we believe is an impartial judgment,"[4] and the resulting convictions are "provisional fixed points which we presume any conception of justice must fix."[5] At the same time, there are some questions on which we lack clear answers, and our aim might be to "remove our doubts."[6] We might want our "principles to accommodate our firmest convictions and to provide guidance where guidance is needed."[7]

We have seen that as Rawls understands the matter, fixed points are only provisionally fixed; we might hold some judgment (say, the death penalty is morally unacceptable) with a great deal of confidence, and we might be exceedingly reluctant to give it up. But we should be willing to consider the possibility that we are wrong. In recent decades, many people opposed same-sex marriage quite firmly, but their judgment shifted, in part because their opposition did not fit well with what else they thought, and with the general principles that they hold.

As Rawls describes the process, "We work from both ends,"[8] involving both abstract principles and judgments about particular cases. If some general principles "match our considered convictions"[9] about those cases, there is no problem. In the case

3. Rawls, 17.
4. Rawls, 18.
5. Rawls, 18.
6. Rawls, 18.
7. Rawls, 18.
8. Rawls, 18.
9. Rawls, 18.

of discrepancies, we might "revise our existing judgments" about particular cases, "for even the judgments that we take provisionally as fixed points are liable to revision."[10] We go back and forth between principles and judgments. When we produce "principles which match our considered judgments duly pruned and adjusted," we are in "reflective equilibrium," defined as such because "our principles and judgments coincide," and because "we know to what principles our judgments conform and the premises of their derivation."[11]

To be sure, the equilibrium might not be *stable*. It might be upset if, for example, reflection "lead[s] us to revise our judgments."[12] It is important to emphasize that on Rawls's account, a "conception of justice cannot be deduced from self-evident premises or conditions on principles"; it is a matter "of everything fitting together into one coherent view."[13] And importantly, Rawls suggests that we consult "our considered convictions at all levels of generality; no one level, say that of abstract principle or that of particular judgments in particular cases, is viewed as foundational. They all may have an initial credibility."[14]

Rawls's motivation was "the hypothesis that the principles which would be chosen in the original position are identical with those that match our considered judgments and so these principles describe our sense of justice."[15] But Rawls urges that this view is too simple, because our considered judgments might be wrong. They might be "subject to certain irregularities

10. Rawls, 18.
11. Rawls, 18.
12. Rawls, 18.
13. Rawls, 19.
14. John Rawls, *Political Liberalism* (1993), 8n8.
15. Rawls, *Theory of Justice*, 42.

and distortions."[16] (Recall that Rawls was speaking of justice, not constitutional law; we will get to the latter very soon.) We might think that meat-eating is acceptable, or that meat-eating is not acceptable, and we cannot know whether we should continue to think that until we test the proposition against our other judgments. When we are given "an intuitively appealing account" of what justice requires, we may well revise our "judgments to conform to its principles even though the theory does not fit" our existing judgments exactly.[17]

We might do this if, for example, we can identify "an explanation for the deviations"[18] that undermines our confidence in our original judgments, and if we can now accept a new judgment. Rawls urges that "from the standpoint of moral philosophy, the best account of a person's sense of justice is not the one which fits his judgments prior to his examining any conception of justice, but rather the one which matches his judgments in reflective equilibrium."[19]

Rawls emphasizes that "a person's sense of justice may or may not undergo a radical shift."[20] He also emphasizes that it may be very difficult to reach reflective equilibrium. To put all of our judgments at every level into order, after consulting "all philosophically relevant arguments,"[21] might be quite challenging. Still, we do our best.[22]

16. Rawls, 42.
17. Rawls, 42.
18. Rawls, 43.
19. Rawls, 43.
20. Rawls, 43.
21. Rawls, 43.
22. There is, of course, a great deal of philosophical work on the search for reflective equilibrium. See, e.g., Norman Daniels, *Justice and Justification* (1996); Sem de Maagt, Reflective Equilibrium and Moral Objectivity, *Inquiry* 60 (2016): 443;

Rawls also distinguishes between two kinds of reflective equilibrium: narrow and wide.[23] We might go back and forth between some judgment about a particular case (say, infanticide is wrong) and a moral principle that seems to justify it (say, it is always wrong to kill a human being). We might think of variations on the case: self-defense, war, assassination of a tyrannical foreign leader, abortion, capital punishment. We might investigate and refine the principle in light of those variations. Eventually we will know what we think of a host of similar cases and potentially supporting principles. If so, we have achieved narrow reflective equilibrium.

With wide reflective equilibrium, we think more broadly. We expose our beliefs to a range of abstract moral *theories*: deontology, utilitarianism, Aristotelian approaches. Rawls's own interest was in wide reflective equilibrium. In Norman Daniels's influential account, wide reflective equilibrium is "a method that attempts to produce coherence in ordered triple sets of beliefs held by a particular person, namely: (a) a set of considered moral judgments, (b) a set of moral principles, and (c) a set of relevant (scientific and philosophical) background theories."[24]

Norman Daniels, "Reflective Equilibrium" (2016), available at https://plato.stanford .edu/entries/reflective-equilibrium/. For present purposes, it is not necessary to explore the details, interesting though they are.

23. See John Rawls, The Independence of Moral Theory, *Proceedings and Addresses of the American Philosophical Association* 48 (1974–75). Rawls does not make the distinction in *A Theory of Justice*, though he does elsewhere. See John Rawls, *Justice as Fairness: A Restatement* (2001). Norman Daniels has developed the distinction in detail. See Norman Daniels, Wide Reflective Equilibrium and Theory Acceptance in Ethics, *Journal of Philosophy* 76 (1979): 256; Daniels, Reflective Equilibrium and Archimedian Points, *Canadian Journal of Philosophy* 10 (1980): 83; Daniels, On Some Methods of Ethics and Linguistics, *Philosophical Studies* 37 (1980): 21.

24. Norman Daniels, "Wide Reflective Equilibrium," 141.

In discussions about what morality requires, the search for reflective equilibrium should be familiar. You might think that polygamy is wrong; how do you square that belief with your belief in a right to marry? You might think that the government can ban Holocaust denial; how do you square that belief with your belief in freedom of speech? You might be drawn to utilitarianism; does that mean that you would strangle a child, if that is the only way to save a village? Utilitarianism might be inconsistent with judgments about particular cases that operate as provisional fixed points, and it might ultimately be rejected for that reason.[25] You might be drawn to Kantianism and insist that people should be treated with respect, and as ends rather than means, whatever the consequences; does that mean that you would not lie, even when that it is the only way to divert a terrorist? Kantianism might also be inconsistent with judgments about particular cases that operate as provisional fixed points, and it might be revised or rejected for that reason.[26]

There has been a great deal of recent discussion about people's moral judgments about particular cases, and about whether they should operate as fixed points. It is possible that they should not be. Behavioral scientists suggest that our judgments often go wrong. We might, for example, show "optimistic bias," and hence think that risks will not come to fruition when we really

25. See J.J.C. Smart and Bernard Williams, *Utilitarianism: For and Against* (1973); Williams's essay is a case study in this approach, and it is worthwhile to consider it in the context of Joshua D. Greene, Beyond Point-and-Shoot Morality, *Ethics* 124 (2014): 695.

26. There is also moral particularism, embodied (roughly) in the view that judgments about particular cases deserve priority and that we should not search for reflective equilibrium. See Jonathan Dancy, Moral Particularism, in *Stanford Encyclopedia of Philosophy*, https://plato.stanford.edu/entries/moral-particularism. There is no analogy (I hope) in constitutional theory.

ought to worry over them. We might show "present bias," and focus on the short term even though we are subject to serious dangers in the long term. Moral judgments about particular cases might be similarly biased. But let us bracket that point for now (or at least reserve it to a long footnote).[27]

27. A growing body of neuroscientific and psychological work is consistent with the view that deontological judgments stem from a moral heuristic, one that works automatically and rapidly. See Greene, "Beyond Point-and-Shoot Morality," 695. It bears emphasizing that if this view is correct, it is also possible—indeed, likely—that such judgments generally work well, in the sense that they produce the right results (according to the appropriate standard) in most cases. The judgments that emerge from automatic processing, including emotional varieties, usually turn out the way they do for a reason. If deontological judgments result from a moral heuristic, we may end up concluding that they generally work well, but that they misfire in systematic ways. See Cass R. Sunstein, Is Deontology a Heuristic? On Psychology, Neuroscience, Ethics, and Law, Iyyun 63 (2014): 83.

Consider in this regard the long-standing philosophical debate over two well-known moral dilemmas, which seem to test deontology and consequentialism. The first, called the trolley problem, asks people to imagine that a runaway trolley is headed for five people, who will be killed if the trolley continues on its current course. The question is whether you would throw a switch that would move the trolley onto another set of tracks, killing one person rather than five. Most people would throw the switch. The second, called the footbridge problem, is the same as that just given, but with one difference: the only way to save the five is to throw a stranger, now on a footbridge that spans the tracks, into the path of the trolley, killing that stranger but preventing the trolley from reaching the others. Most people will not kill the stranger.

What is the difference between the two cases, if any? A great deal of philosophical work has been done on this question, much of it trying to suggest that our firm intuitions can indeed be defended, or rescued, as a matter of principle. The basic idea seems to be that those firm intuitions, separating the two cases, tell us something important about what morality requires, and an important philosophical task is to explain why they are essentially right. Without engaging these arguments, consider a simpler answer. As a matter of principle, there is no difference between the two cases. People's different reactions are based on a deontological heuristic ("Do not throw innocent people to their death") that condemns the throwing of the stranger but not the throwing of the switch. To say the least, it is desirable for people to act

Interpretation and Fixed Points

Are there fixed points in constitutional law? How provisional are they? Are they abstract (say, the rule of law) or are they particular (say, sex discrimination is forbidden)? How do they bear, and how should they bear, on our judgments about the appropriate approach to constitutional interpretation? Is there an analogue to the search for reflective equilibrium in constitutional theory, acknowledging that the purpose of the latter is not to produce a theory of justice? In constitutional law, how should we understand the idea of fixed points?

In the United States, many people would refuse to accept a theory of constitutional interpretation that leads to the conclusion that *Brown v. Board of Education*[28] was wrongly decided. If a proposed theory would allow racial segregation by state governments, the theory would (in their view) have to be rejected. The reason, in short, is that a constitutional order that allowed racial segregation would be intolerably unjust, and we should be reluctant to interpret the Constitution in such a way

---

on the basis of a moral heuristic that makes it extremely abhorrent to use physical force to kill innocent people. But the underlying heuristic misfires in drawing a distinction between the two ingeniously devised cases. Hence, people (including philosophers) struggle heroically to rescue their intuitions and to establish that the two cases are genuinely different in principle. But they are not. If they are not, then a deontological intuition is serving as a heuristic in the footbridge problem, and it is leading people in the wrong direction.

If it is, a serious question might be raised about the idea of seeking reflective equilibrium in moral and political philosophy. Some of our moral intuitions are indeed very firm, and their firmness may be a good thing (because it has good consequences), but perhaps they misfire, and perhaps we should be willing to reconsider them, at least if the result would be to produce more accuracy (in the form of better consequences) than can result from a mere heuristic.

28. 347 U.S. 483 (1954).

as to allow our constitutional order to be intolerably unjust (unless we are absolutely required to do so). So long as a theory of interpretation is optional, and so long as a relevant constitutional provision can be interpreted to forbid intolerable injustice, we should hesitate to adopt a theory that would allow such injustice. What is taken as intolerably unjust by some is not so taken by others, which helps explain why different people have different fixed points.

In the same vein, many other people would refuse to accept a theory of interpretation that is inconsistent with *Bolling v. Sharpe*,[29] which ruled that the federal government is not permitted to segregate the schools in the District of Columbia. As a matter of constitutional law, *Bolling* was a hard case. In segregating schools, what provision of the Constitution did Congress violate? Was racial segregation by the federal government unconstitutional in, say, 1795? In 1850? In 1890? If not, why in 1954? The Fourteenth Amendment, which contains the Equal Protection Clause, applies only to the states, not to the national government; no general equality provision applies to Congress. It is challenging indeed, on originalist or even textualist grounds, to defend the argument that the national government is forbidden from mandating racial segregation. In making that argument in 1954, the Supreme Court invoked the Due Process Clause of the Fifth Amendment, which forbids the federal government from depriving any person of life, liberty, or property "without due process of law." But when it was ratified in 1791, did the Due Process Clause forbid racial segregation? Certainly not. In any case, the Due Process Clause seems to guarantee process (of some kind); it does not appear to forbid discrimination at all.

29. 347 U.S. 497 (1954).

In *Bolling*, the Supreme Court announced that the federal government cannot, in fact, segregate schools on the basis of race. Here is what the Court said:

> The Fifth Amendment, which is applicable in the District of Columbia, does not contain an equal protection clause, as does the Fourteenth Amendment, which applies only to the states. But the concepts of equal protection and due process, both stemming from our American ideal of fairness, are not mutually exclusive. The "equal protection of the laws" is a more explicit safeguard of prohibited unfairness than "due process of law," and therefore we do not imply that the two are always interchangeable phrases. But, as this Court has recognized, discrimination may be so unjustifiable as to be violative of due process. . . . Segregation in public education is not reasonably related to any proper governmental objective, and thus it imposes on Negro children of the District of Columbia a burden that constitutes an arbitrary deprivation of their liberty in violation of the Due Process Clause. In view of our decision that the Constitution prohibits the states from maintaining racially segregated public schools, it would be unthinkable that the same Constitution would impose a lesser duty on the Federal Government.

Purely as a matter of textualism, *Bolling* is exceedingly difficult to defend. The Due Process Clause of the Fifth Amendment certainly does not read like a prohibition on discrimination on the basis of race. As a matter of originalism, *Bolling* is indeed impossible to defend. Semantic originalists would have real trouble making sense of the Court's ruling. For those who emphasize original intentions or original public meaning, *Bolling* is preposterous. The decision is best seen as a moral reading. Notice the

word "unthinkable"? That is a giveaway that the Court is thinking in moral terms.

Bolling is not an isolated decision. Over the decades, it has
come to stand for a large proposition: The Due Process Clause
contains an "equal protection component," which means that
the federal government is essentially subject to the constraints
of the Equal Protection Clause, whether it is discriminating on
the basis of race, sex, citizenship, sexual orientation, or any
other ground. Textualists struggle to accept that set of rulings.
Originalists cannot possibly accept that set of rulings. Was *Bolling* wrong? Are the cases that follow it wrong? Should they be
overruled? Judges (and the rest of us) would seem to have a
choice: Accept *Bolling* and successor cases, and forbid discrimination by the national government, and reject originalism;[30]
or reject *Bolling* and successor cases, and allow discrimination
by the national government, and accept originalism. There is no
obvious alternative.[31]

---

30. Things are a bit more complex. An originalist could have a commitment to
stare decisis, and so could say that the cases, though wrong, will not be overruled. I
turn to this point below. The claim in the text is that a host of foundational cases
must, on originalist grounds, be taken to have been wrongly decided. Is that a problem? I think so.

31. Alert to the difficulty of defending *Bolling* in its own terms, some people have
urged that the outcome might be justified by reference to the Citizenship Clause of
the Fourteenth Amendment. That Clause reads as follows: "All persons born or naturalized in the United States, and subject to the jurisdiction thereof, are citizens of the
United States and of the State wherein they reside." The obvious (and minimal)
function of the Citizenship Clause is to overrule *Dred Scott*: regardless of skin color
or race, those who are born or naturalized in the United States count as citizens. At
first glance, the Citizenship Clause does not create an independent or freestanding
equality principle. At second glance, it is not easily read to create an independent or
freestanding equality principle, for one simple reason: it is followed in short order
by the Equal Protection Clause. If the Citizenship Clause already imposes an equality
requirement, what is the Equal Protection Clause doing there?

Here is one view: If a proposed theory of interpretation would allow the national government to discriminate on the basis of race, that is a real problem for the theory, or so many people would conclude. (I agree with them.) Or suppose that a proposed theory of interpretation would allow the states or the national government to discriminate on the basis of sex, or that it would result in a modest understanding of the right to freedom of speech, one that would allow suppression of political dissent. Many people would seriously doubt or even reject the theory for that reason. (I agree with them.)

We need to underline a point here about the difference between constitutional law and political morality. I am speaking of judgments that are fixed points in the sense that many people will find it extremely difficult to accept a theory of *constitutional*

We might be able to reduce the problem of redundancy if we emphasize that the Equal Protection Clause was understood as an effort, not to create a general *equality* principle, but to solve the specific problem of unequal *protection* of the laws—for example, the authorities protecting white people, but not Black people, from criminal violence. But even if that view is plausible (and it is), then the Privileges or Immunities Clause, and not the Citizenship Clause, is more naturally taken as the general antidiscrimination principle of the Fourteenth Amendment: "No State shall make or enforce any law which shall abridge the privileges or immunities of citizens of the United States." The Privileges or Immunities Clause, of course, applies only to the states. For this reason, it is reasonable (1) to take the Citizenship Clause as establishing only what it purports to establish, and not to serve as a general source of substantive rights or as a general equality principle; (2) to take the Equal Protection Clause as requiring, well, equal protection; and (3) to take the Privileges or Immunities Clause as protecting a set of substantive rights and as forbidding discrimination with respect to their enjoyment.

To be sure, some portions of the relevant debates might be taken to suggest a broader role for the Citizenship Clause, and I do not mean to settle the question with this very compressed discussion. The only point is that it is difficult indeed to defend, all of a sudden and essentially now, the conclusion that the relevant statements are enough to suggest that the Citizenship Clause contains a broad equality guarantee, sufficient to support *Bolling* (let alone its successors).

law that rejects them. But there are many fixed points in political morality that do not count as fixed points for purposes of constitutional law. You might think, for example, that people should not eat meat, that no one should be homeless, that everyone deserves a decent education, that discrimination against the elderly is appalling, and that no one should be hungry, without also thinking that the Constitution has anything to say about these issues. You might embrace Franklin Delano Roosevelt's Second Bill of Rights, recognizing various economic guarantees, without thinking that the Constitution embeds them.[32] To be sure, those who distinguish between fixed points as a matter of constitutional law and fixed points as a matter of political morality need some kind of explanation of why they do so, and moral readers might be challenged to find one. The only point is that in constitutional law, fixed points are present, and they are not merely precedents; they reflect commitments that people would be exceedingly reluctant to give up.

People with different fixed points might emphasize different cases. Suppose that a theory would mean that *District of Columbia v. Heller*, protecting the individual right to possess guns, was incorrectly decided. Many people would conclude that if so, the theory is probably wrong. Some people will think that if a theory suggests that *Brandenburg v. Ohio*, broadly protecting political speech through a version of the "clear and present danger" test, was wrong, the theory must be wrong. Other people will think that if a theory suggests that *Brandenburg v. Ohio* was right, or might be right,[33] we had better find another theory.

32. See Cass R. Sunstein, *The Second Bill of Rights* (2004).

33. There is a lurking question about how much judicial discretion a theory authorizes. A pervasive concern about "moral readings" is that different judges will offer

Simply as a matter of constitutional sociology, it seems plausible to suggest that a commitment to *Brown* and *Bolling* has played a massive role in thinking about the plausibility of theories of constitutional interpretation. Certainty that one or both of these decisions was right, or that some other decision was right or wrong, has helped to motivate and to ground some of those theories. Judges and others are at pains to urge that their preferred theory does not throw (too many, or the wrong) fixed points into history's ashbin. But I am also suggesting that whatever we think of any particular holdings, use of fixed points, in deciding among theories of interpretation, is not merely a matter of constitutional sociology. It is a necessary feature of that decision (a point to which I will return). In this domain, there is no alternative to the search for reflective equilibrium. There is nowhere else to go. It is the only game in town.

One's fixed points (yours!) might not be limited to *existing* rulings. You care about the constitutional future, not merely the constitutional present. You might reject a theory of interpretation that might make space for, or require, a (future) return to *Lochner v. New York*, which struck down maximum hour laws, or anything like it. You might reject a theory of interpretation that might, in the future, allow or require government to restrict political dissent. You might reject a theory of interpretation that puts the administrative state in (future) constitutional jeopardy, and that would (for example) cast constitutional doubt on the Clean Air Act or the Occupational Safety and Health Act.

---

different moral readings. On one moral reading, for example, *Brandenburg* is right; on another, *Brandenburg* is wrong, and states can do as they like; on another, *Brandenburg* is wrong, and states may regulate dangerous speech. An appeal of Thayerism, traditionalism, and originalism is that they promise, or hope, to reduce judicial discretion.

More fundamentally, many people would reject a theory of interpretation that would rule out new and (to us) surprising developments that would expand prevailing conceptions of liberty and equality. They would insist on opening the ground for something like a *Brown v. Board of Education*, or an *Obergefell* (requiring states to recognize same-sex marriage), for new and future generations. They would make a bet, to the effect that history remains wide open, which is a pretty good bet. They would also make a bet that a Supreme Court, operating under a theory that makes space for decisions like *Brown* or *Obergefell*, appropriately expanding equality and liberty, would produce a similar decision in 2030, or 2040, or 2090, also appropriately expanding equality and liberty (not the worst bet, though also perhaps not the best).[34]

What are the candidates here? Anyone can guess, and guesses might seem preposterous and alarming, or preposterous and inspiring. In 1930 it would have seemed pretty adventurous to say that the Equal Protection Clause would be understood to forbid racial segregation; but by 1954, there we were. In 1950 it would have seemed pretty wild to say that discrimination on the basis of sex would be seen as a violation of the Equal Protection Clause; but by 1980, there we were. As late as 2000 it would have been reckless, and maybe absurd, to suggest that the Supreme Court might recognize a right to same-sex marriage; but in 2015, that is exactly what happened. And, of course, the constitutional pendulum swings in multiple directions. You might applaud an unanticipated development; you might deplore it.

---

34. Some people would, of course, believe that to be a terrible bet, on institutional grounds. They might believe that the democratic process would and should make any expansions. They might believe that judicial expansions, as the judges might see it, would likely be grave mistakes.

The left and the right will, of course, applaud and deplore different rulings, and anticipated reactions play a significant role in judgments about the appropriate theory of interpretation. (With a right-of-center Supreme Court, it should be no wonder that progressives are now drawn to Thayerism and to popular constitutionalism.)

Would it be adventurous or reckless to suggest that by 2040 we might see constitutional rights that can only be imagined, or barely be imagined, today? Actually it would be adventurous and reckless to suggest that we will *not* see those things.

Suppose that someone proposes a theory of interpretation that is consistent with all, or almost all, of the relevant fixed points, taken as part of the fabric of existing constitutional law. (Your own fixed points, for example.) Would you be inclined to accept that theory? In part for that very reason? If so, would you be right to do so, or would you be unprincipled, or engaged in a form of special pleading? My suggestion here is that you would be right to do so, and not unprincipled in the least, even as you would be open to counterarguments.

Note that there is a large and critical difference between one's fixed points and one's preferred results. There are many more of the latter than the former. You might want the Supreme Court to issue certain rulings, but if it does not, you will think it reasonable, and even if you think it unreasonable, you might not think that something horrible or horrific has happened. A theory of constitutional law might not yield *all* of one's preferred results (it had better not), but it might also yield, or at least not foreclose, all, most, or many of one's fixed points. Note as well that I am suggesting that for judges (or others) thinking about theories of constitutional interpretation, the relevant fixed points really are, and must be, their own. One judge might think that if *Griswold*, protecting the right of married couples to use contraceptives, turns out to be wrong, it is not really so bad; another judge might think that same thing about *Bolling v. Sharpe*. Others might disagree. And it is important to see that we are not speaking of a small number of fixed points or a handful of iconic cases; a theory of interpretation might well be acceptable if it undoes just a few. The real problem comes if such a theory operates as a wrecking ball (as Thayerism would, and as, in my view, consistent use of the original public meaning would).

Of course, it is also true that judges should be humble, and they might be concerned to ensure that their own fixed points are not idiosyncratic. They might defer to the wisdom of the legal culture in taking some decisions, and not others, as fixed points.

Theories, Again

Return in this light to the idea, associated with James Bradley Thayer, that the Court should uphold legislation unless it is clearly and unambiguously unconstitutional. Thayer embraced the view that "an Act of the legislature is not to be declared void unless the violation of the constitution is so manifest as to leave no room for reasonable doubt." As we have seen, Thayerism is not a complete theory of interpretation. To apply it, we need to know what the Constitution means, so that we can see whether the violation is "so manifest as to leave no room for reasonable doubt." But many people would conclude, on reflection, that when reasonably completed, Thayerism would lead to intolerable results in countless many cases. It would likely require rejection of *Brown*, *Bolling*, and *Heller*, for example, and it would also certainly lead to the conclusion that state and federal governments can discriminate on the basis of sex. It would obliterate the right to freedom of speech, as that right is now understood. Is this a decisive argument against across-the-board Thayerism? Very possibly. (I think so.) The question is the relative fixity of the fixed points inconsistent with Thayerism—of how fixed they are, exactly.

Or consider traditionalism, captured in the view that some, many, or all constitutional rights must be able to point to long-standing traditions in their favor.[35] Due process traditionalism would be inconsistent with a large number of modern substantive due process cases, including *Lawrence*, banning criminal prohibitions on same-sex relations, and *Obergefell*. (Much more on that in chapter 5.) Some people would be strongly disinclined to accept due process traditionalism for that very reason. (Chapter 5 supports them.)

One question is whether the skeptics might nonetheless be prepared to accept due process traditionalism, perhaps on the ground that existing decisions, including *Lawrence* and *Obergefell*, would be "grandfathered"—that is, would be allowed to stand as existing precedents—even if the Court would not extend them, or go beyond traditions in the future. If the skeptics would not be content with that approach, it might be because they believe that grandfathering is not enough, and that a general principle of liberty, not confined by tradition and not limited to existing cases, is the appropriate foundation for constitutional law. (I agree with them again.)[36]

---

35. Washington v. Glucksberg, 521 U.S. 702, 720–21 (1997); Michael H. v. Gerald D., 491 U.S. 110, 122–24 (1989); Moore v. City of E. Cleveland, 431 U.S. 494, 503 (1977).

36. I am trying to keep the argument simple and straightforward, but occasionally that is a bit of a struggle. If judges who departed from traditions created bogus rights, or horrific rights (a right to torture animals?), we might favor traditionalism. The paragraph in the text depends on some optimistic hunches about what judges will

For its part, equal protection traditionalism does not seem at all promising, in part because it would be inconsistent with so many fixed points.[37] Actually, equal protection traditionalism seems terrible. The Equal Protection Clause is a challenge to existing traditions, not an effort to protect them. Discrimination on the basis of sex is not exactly inconsistent with longstanding traditions.

Turn now to originalism. As we have seen, that idea can be understood in many different ways, and I bracket the differences here. There is a fair argument that modern forms of originalism would throw a great deal of existing constitutional law into doubt, or into the ashcan. It might well mean, for example, that both *Brown* and *Bolling* were wrong; that the national government can discriminate on the basis of both race and sex; that the Due Process Clause of the Fifth Amendment is a narrow concept and does not even require "procedural due process"[38] (that is, the right to a fair hearing); and that the First Amendment does not forbid governments from imposing what they

---

or would actually do. If those hunches are wrong, traditionalism or Thayerism would look a lot better. I make this point in various places below.

37. This is a compressed version of what might have to be an extended argument. One reason is that many originalists urge, more than plausibly, that the constitutional source of a general equality principle is the Privileges or Immunities Clause, and its scope raises many puzzles. For a valuable, provocative discussion, see Randy Barnett and Evan Bernick, *The Original Meaning of the Fourteenth Amendment* (2021). Would privileges or immunities traditionalism be appealing? Probably not, because it would be inconsistent with so many fixed points. Note that privileges or immunities originalism may or may not turn out to be traditionalist; everything depends on the right conception of originalism and what historical inquiry reveals.

38. For an illuminating and in some ways startling discussion, see Lawrence B. Solum and Max Crema, The Original Meaning of "Due Process of Law" in the Fifth Amendment, *Va. L. Rev.* 108 (2022).

deem to be reasonable regulation on speech.[39] If so, what follows? My suggestion here is straightforward: It follows that originalism is wrong.

The Challenge of Fixed Points

Originalists have several answers to this objection. First, they might be willing to bite plenty of bullets. They might argue that the relevant fixed points should be taken as only provisionally fixed, and that if they become unfixed as a result of the correct theory of interpretation, so be it. It is not easy to swallow the idea that *Brown* was wrong, but some originalists would be willing to do exactly that. They might not enjoy it, but they might be willing to say that if they have to choose between *Brown* and originalism, the choice is not really hard. They might ask: Why should intuitions, and in particular moral intuitions, be given decisive weight when it comes to constitutional law?

Second, they might argue that some or many of the fixed points are actually preserved by originalism.[40] Originalists have in fact been at great pains to make that argument in several domains and especially with respect to *Brown*. They contend that if we look hard enough at the history, we will find that the

---

39. See Jud Campbell, "Natural Rights and the First Amendment," *Yale Law Journal* 127 (2017): 246–321.

40. See Barnett and Bernick, *The Original Meaning*, 19–21, and, in particular, these words: "Finally, getting the original meaning of the Fourteenth Amendment right helps legitimate originalism itself. Nonoriginalists have trotted out a litany of entrenched constitutional doctrines that most Americans celebrate but are said to be contrary to the original meaning of the text. These critics then urge that this conflict between popular moral intuitions and originalism should be resolved against originalism. If, however, originalism not only fits but morally justifies popular doctrines, then there is no conflict to resolve" (21). For a vivid illustration, see United States v. Vaello Madero, 142 S.Ct. 1539 (2022) (Thomas, J., concurring in the judgment).

original public meaning of the Fourteenth Amendment is, in fact, consistent with *Brown*, and indeed with a large number of decisions that nonoriginalists fear would be endangered by originalism. They argue, in brief, that originalism is not so bad, in terms of the results that it encourages or requires. Actually, they say, it is pretty good.[41]

In fact, we can find an important strand of thinking that we might call "progressive originalism," which does battle on originalist terrain, but which argues that, properly understood, originalism leads to progressive results. In an oral argument in 2022, Justice Ketanji Brown Jackson offered an originalist argument in favor of affirmative action:[42]

So I looked at the report that was submitted by the Joint Committee on Reconstruction, which drafted the Fourteenth Amendment, and that report says that the entire point of the amendment was to secure rights of the freed former slaves. The legislator who introduced that amendment said that "unless the Constitution should restrain them, those states will all, I fear, keep up this discrimination and crush to death the hated freedmen." That's not—that's not a race-neutral or race-blind idea in terms of the remedy. . . . I don't think that the historical record establishes that the founders believed that race neutrality or race blindness was required, right? . . . And, importantly, when there was a concern that the Civil Rights Act wouldn't have a constitutional foundation, that's when the Fourteenth Amendment came into play. It was drafted to give a foundational—a constitutional foundation

41. See Barnett and Bernick, *The Original Meaning*.

42. See Transcript of Oral Argument at 57–59, Merrill v. Milligan (No. 21-1086), available at https://www.supremecourt.gov/oral_arguments/argument_transcripts/2022/21-1086_f204.pdf.

for a piece of legislation that was designed to make people who had less opportunity and less rights equal to white citizens.

We can see this argument as representative of an assortment of arguments that originalism will often lead to results that will please progressives.[43] Right-of-center theorists, committed to originalism, may or may not agree with those arguments, but they will welcome them: At least they identify the terrain on which arguments should be occurring. It is a fair question whether we should think of progressive constitutionalism as mostly strategic—as a response to the increased authority of originalism in the Supreme Court. The basic point is that when confronted with fixed points, defenders of originalism, whatever their politics, might say: *You don't have so much to worry about.*

Third, originalists might argue that they are committed to respect for precedent, which would mean that the fixed points would be preserved. (A "go forth and sin no more" approach to constitutional law.)

Fourth, they might argue that a central advantage of original-ism is its neutrality; the results that it requires do not depend on the judges' views about particular cases. If some of those results are deplorable, well, in a sense that is something to be proud of. In any case, democracy (and not free-form judicial scrutiny) is always a backstop, and perhaps the right and the best safeguard, against deplorable results. If we want to protect new rights, we should do that through politics, not through the courts: the Americans with Disabilities Act, enacted by Congress, sure; a made-up constitutional right to be free from discrimination on the basis of disability, absolutely not.

---

43. Barnett and Bernick, in *The Original Meaning*, offer many such arguments.

Fifth, originalists might argue that their approach is mandatory and the only real fixed point,[44] which means that if it
requires abhorrent conclusions, that is, in a sense, a badge of
honor.[45] On one view, originalism is the only legitimate approach
to interpretation, justified independently of the outcomes that it
produces; whether it leads to rejection of provisional fixed points
is (well) entirely beside the point. And on this view, it is crucial
to reiterate that fixed points in constitutional law, as in moral
and political philosophy, operate at multiple levels of generality.
One or another approach might turn out to *be* the fixed point.
Or one or another moral value—the rule of law, democratic
self-government, stability and predictability, some conception
of liberty—might turn out, for some or many, to be the relevant
fixed point. One or more of those values might support
originalism.

Each of these responses must be considered separately. It is
noteworthy that some originalists appear to find it important
to establish that their preferred approach would not endanger

44. Compare Barnett and Bernick, *The Original Meaning*, 280: "Besides, in many,
if not most, cases, we do not start with normative priors. . . . We think that theoretical
arguments in favor of originalism . . . not whether originalism produces outcomes
that fit one's normative priors, are the better way."

45. Compare Barnett and Bernick, *The Original Meaning*, 280: "We resist the
modern tendency to justify methods of interpretation based solely on whether
they produce normatively attractive results. We need to identify an interpretive
method that will accurately determine what the law *is* before we can figure out
what we can figure out what public officials *ought* to do about it." Do we? Maybe
so; in some sense, surely so. But return to the search for reflective equilibrium,
and note that use of the original public meaning, as the right approach to interpretation, cannot be justified (without circularity) on the ground that it is the
only way to determine, "accurately," what the law is. See Ronald Dworkin, *Law's
Empire* (1985). In a relevant (and not colloquial) sense, constitutional law is not
rocket science.

(too) many fixed points—principally by urging that the approach authorizes or requires them,[46] but sometimes by pointing to the potential importance of stare decisis, and sometimes by suggesting that even if some fixed points should be unfixed, democracy will handle the problem. Originalists rightly say that it is a strong point in favor of *any* approach to constitutional law if it ensures that results will not depend on the judges' personal views about particular cases.[47] (Thayerians say that too.) The challenge, of course, is to square that kind of neutrality with (appropriate) respect for fixed points.

Does originalism preserve fixed points? Does it preserve enough of them? My main goal here is to say that these are important questions to ask, and that originalism stands or falls on the answers. I agree with Justice Jackson on the Fourteenth Amendment; it does not forbid affirmative action programs on originalist grounds, and it is genuinely shocking that justices who are committed to originalism have voted to strike down such programs. (Justices Scalia and Thomas are examples.) But whatever we think of affirmative action, I hope to have shown that public meaning originalism fails to preserve too many fixed points. Perhaps I am wrong. If originalists reject that conclusion, that is an excellent conversation to have.

It is good, of course, if originalists are willing to say that while their approach would not justify (say) *Brown* and *Bolling* in the first instance, they are committed to respect for precedent, and so would not overrule those and other decisions. Are

46. See, e.g., Michael W. McConnell, Originalism and the Desegregation Decisions, *Va. L. Rev.* 81 (1995): 947, 955–84; Barnett and Bernick, *The Original Meaning*.

47. It is fair to ask to what extent this is possible. See Frank Cross, *The Failed Promise of Originalism* (2013).

precedent-respecting originalists able to preserve enough fixed points? Maybe so. If so, we should applaud them. We would also have to discuss the arc of constitutional law, and ask whether, for the next ten years, or thirty years, or fifty years, originalism would be better than the alternatives. I offer a provisional no to that question (see chapter 5). The answer is provisional because a great deal depends on judgments about institutional capacities—about who is good at what, and about who is likely to do what.

Is democracy a backstop? In some ways, of course it is. Married couples probably need not fear that they will be forbidden to use contraceptives. It is not likely that states are going to try to sterilize those convicted of crimes. Over the course of American history, the Supreme Court's aggressive role, grounded in what a majority of the justices considered a moral reading, has sometimes been something to abhor. One reason is that the Court has prohibited the democratic process from correcting wrongs; consider decisions entrenching slavery, striking down maximum hour and minimum wage laws, and invalidating campaign finance laws. A Thayerian Supreme Court would have allowed the democratic process to do a number of good things (on moral grounds). Over the course of the next century, maybe the democratic process would do the good things that an aggressive Supreme Court would do—and thus make an aggressive Supreme Court less necessary. Any judgment on that topic would be speculative in the extreme.

Of the various responses, the most complicated is the fifth, to the effect that originalism is mandatory and so the only truly fixed point. To evaluate that claim, we need to specify the right conception of originalism; which kind is mandatory? In chapter 2 we saw that whatever kind of originalism we specify, it is a choice, and it has to be defended on some ground. We might choose to interpret the words of the Constitution in accordance with the "original intentions" of the ratifiers; that is an admissible understanding of interpretation. We might choose to interpret the words of the Constitution in accordance with the original public meaning, understood with contextual enrichment; that is an admissible understanding of interpretation. One more time: Whether we should make that choice, or some other, depends on what would make our constitutional order better rather than worse. There is no escaping that question, and fixed points are relevant to the answer.

To see the problem, consider some analogies. Here is the bat-and-ball problem: *A baseball bat and a ball cost $1.10 together, and the bat costs $1.00 more than the ball. How much does the bat cost?* Most people answer $1. The correct answer is $1.05. Even if the $1 answer is a kind of fixed point, the right answer is $1.05. Or consider the view that the correct spelling of the word "accommodate" is actually "accomodate"; that is a mistake, even if one holds that view very firmly. Or consider the view that the word "unique" means "unusual," as opposed to (well) "unique." A person might be firmly convinced of her mistake, but it is still a mistake.

Constitutional interpretation is different. There is nothing that interpretation just is. We might embrace Thayerism on democratic grounds, or traditionalism on Burkean grounds, or originalism on rule-of-law grounds. It is open to originalists to contend that the grounds that justify their preferred approach (the rule of law, stability, feasible constitutional law amidst pluralism) outweigh everything else, including some admittedly terrible outcomes in some cases. The only point is that such grounds have to be spelled out, and those who favor one or another approach have to anticipate and offer convincing responses to counterarguments. In that process, fixed points of one or another sort are crucial.

This is not at all a claim that the choice among theories of interpretation is arbitrary or a matter of whim. It is anything but that. But as in moral and political philosophy, so too here: in choosing among such theories, we cannot possibly ignore or refuse to attend to fixed points, even if they are subject to revision. I am emphasizing fixed points about particular cases, but as I have said, fixed points can operate at many levels of generality. Recall that a conception of self-government might turn out to be a crucial fixed point.

Each chooser—each one of us—must make a judgment about what those fixed points are, about exactly how fixed they are, and about whether one or another approach would endanger them. For some people, the correctness of *Brown* is a fixed point, and any theory that rejects *Brown* must be rejected for that reason. For other people, that conclusion is too strong. For some people, there would be nothing disturbing about the conclusion that *Griswold v. Connecticut* was wrong, and nothing particularly disturbing, even, about the conclusion that *Griswold* must be overruled. For other people, such a conclusion would be exceptionally troubling.

It is important to reiterate that a theory of interpretation would not be unacceptable if it leads to *some* bad consequences, including unfixing *some* fixed points, if its overall consequences are good.[48] Indeed, any theory of interpretation had better lead

---

48. The following sentence seems to me entirely correct: "An interpretive method that gives us less of what we might normatively want than a rival method in a given case might appear normatively deficient until we recognize that it is more likely to promote the rule of law in a pluralistic society than its rival." Barnett and Bernick, *The Original Meaning*, 380. I would add only that even though the rule of law is an exceedingly important value, it is not the only one, and different theories of interpretation might promote that value in different ways and to different degrees. (I do not think that Barnett and Bernick would disagree.)

to some bad consequences. No one thinks that judges should cure all or even most of society's ills. (Recall Franklin Delano Roosevelt's Second Bill of Rights, which I favor as a guide to legislation;[49] it would be hard to argue that the Second Bill is constitutionally compelled. I favor strong steps to combat the risks associated with climate change, but I do not believe that the Constitution requires those steps.) The suddenly doubtful validity of some provisional fixed points is necessarily a problem, but it is not necessarily a decisive objection to a theory of interpretation. Whether it is one or the other depends on what we lose from it and what we gain from it. It is not possible to choose a theory of interpretation without making a judgment on those questions, even if that judgment depends on a degree of speculation about institutional capacities—about who is good at what.

By way of summary, let us bring some of these points down to earth. In the abstract, many people are drawn to Thayerism, on the ground that it is highly respectful of the democratic process. In our world, however, it would be intolerable; it would lead to an unduly truncated system of rights and liberties. In the abstract, many people are drawn to traditionalism. The question is whether it would tear at the fabric of too much of American constitutional law (see chapter 5). In the abstract, many

---

I might add, parenthetically, that if Barnett and Bernick are correct about the content of the original understanding of the Fourteenth Amendment, the argument for originalism as they understand it gains a great deal of strength—in significant part because originalism, on their view of what it requires, does not compromise (many of what seem to me to be) fixed points. (At least this is so of Fourteenth Amendment originalism.) I should add that on their view as I understand it, fixed points are essentially beside the point; I admire their book, but, as should be clear, I disagree with them on that question.

49. See Sunstein, *The Second Bill of Rights* (2004).

people are drawn to originalism. The question is what it would produce or entail. In my view, democracy-reinforcing judicial review is a terrific foundation for modern constitutional law. I have not demonstrated that point here, but I hope that I have identified the grounds on which it might not be found convincing. To get more clarity on those grounds, let us now look more closely at traditionalism, which seems to have growing appeal within the Supreme Court of the United States.

5

Traditions: "Athwart History, Yelling Stop"

WE CAN find traditionalism in many places in current constitutional law, including protection of Second Amendment rights,
freedom of speech, religious liberty, and separation of powers. We
can find it, too, in the Court's decision to overrule *Roe v. Wade*.
Indeed, respect for tradition is on the ascendancy. The current
Supreme Court is often an originalist court, but much of the time
it is a traditionalist court. As we have seen, the two are close, but
they are not the same. We might note at the outset that originalism
and traditionalism share something in common: They hope to
limit judicial discretion, and they seek to ensure that judges will
speak for the values and commitments of others, not themselves.
They hope to reduce the risk of judicial tyranny, whatever its form.
They are also backward-looking, which is part of their appeal.

Traditionalism is nothing new. (Which is good news for traditionalists.) Its roots lie in American traditions. In his dissenting opinion in *Lochner v. New York*, striking down a maximum
hour law, Justice Holmes wrote that the Due Process Clause
would be violated only if "a rational and fair man necessarily
would admit that the statute proposed would infringe

fundamental principles as they have been understood by the traditions of our people and our law."[1] To that extent, Holmes was a traditionalist, He urged that if a law infringed fundamental principles, defined by traditions, it would be unconstitutional. We have seen that Holmes was first and foremost a Thayerian, but he offered an exception for situations in which a legislature infringed on tradition—as it might if, for example, it adopted a "one family, one child" rule for heterosexual couples, or if it banned heterosexual marriage.

In the same vein, Justice Frankfurter, also a Thayerian, explicitly urged that in assessing due process questions, courts should ask whether proceedings "offend those canons of decency and fairness which express the notions of justice of English-speaking peoples."[2] Frankfurter cherished those canons of decency and fairness. Built up over time, they reflected, in his view, a stock of wisdom and reason. If a legislature offended them, it would run into serious constitutional trouble.

In 1955, William F. Buckley Jr., the influential conservative thinker, wrote of his then-new magazine, *National Review*: "It stands athwart history, yelling Stop." Traditionalists do exactly that. They do so on principle. They believe that traditions are likely to be good, because they reflect the wisdom of numerous people over time and are the opposite of a short-term fad; recall Burke's arguments on behalf of that conclusion. They also believe that efforts to assess traditions are likely to go wrong; recall Burke's emphasis on the limits of the reason of individuals or even of individual generations.

In overruling *Roe v. Wade*, which protected the right to choose abortion, the Court gave pride of place to tradition. Its

1. 198 U.S. 45, 76 (1905) (Holmes, J., dissenting).
2. Rochin v. California, 342 U.S. 165, 169 (1952).

opinion in *Dobbs v. Jackson Women's Health Organization*[3]
makes reference to originalism, but much more than that, it
embraces a kind of due process traditionalism. That commitment is the engine for the Court's understanding of the reach
of "liberty" under the Due Process Clause. My goal in this chapter is to explore that commitment and to identify the grounds
on which we might accept or reject traditionalism. Understanding those grounds will, I hope, go a long way toward clarifying
the choice among theories of interpretation.

To accomplish that goal, we will do a deep dive into *Dobbs*,
not only because of its evident importance but also because
it offers a universe in a grain of sand; it tells us a great deal
about traditionalism and its limits. In my view, we should reject constitutional traditionalism, on the ground that (to put
it too simply) the arc of history bends toward justice. The
Supreme Court had it right when it said this, in the *Obergefell*
decision in 2015, requiring states to recognize same-sex
marriage:[4]

> The nature of injustice is that we may not always see it in our
> own times. The generations that wrote and ratified the Bill
> of Rights and the Fourteenth Amendment did not presume
> to know the extent of freedom in all of its dimensions, and
> so they entrusted to future generations a charter protecting
> the right of all persons to enjoy liberty as we learn its mean-
> ing. When new insight reveals discord between the Constitu-
> tion's central protections and a received legal stricture, a
> claim to liberty must be addressed.

> Amen.

3. Dobbs v. Jackson Women's Health Org., 142 S.Ct. 2228 (2022).
4. Obergefell v. Hodges, 576 U.S. 644, 663 (2015).

Deep Roots

Does the Constitution protect the right to privacy? The right to use contraceptives? The right to same-sex marriage? The right to choose abortion? In *Dobbs*, the Court said that while the Due Process Clause "has been held to guarantee some rights that are not mentioned in the Constitution," its reach is limited to rights that are (1) "deeply rooted in this Nation's history and tradition" *and* (2) "implicit in the concept of ordered liberty." The Court emphasized that the very idea of "substantive due process," by which the Due Process Clause extends beyond procedural guarantees, "has long been controversial." By itself, the text of the Clause seems to suggest a purely procedural interpretation; it reads as if it is focused on processes, not on whether laws are reasonable. It seems to require fair hearings ("due process"). It does not appear, on its face, to give any substantive protection to rights at all.[5] It seems to suggest that people must receive notice before their liberty is taken, without saying that government is flatly prohibited from imposing burdens or restricting freedom. John Hart Ely went so far as to describe substantive due process as "a contradiction in terms—sort of like 'green pastel redness.'"[6]

While recognizing that substantive due process has been controversial, the Court acknowledged that the Court's decisions have protected two categories of substantive rights. Both categories are, in the Court's view, to be understood directly by

---

5. To textualists and originalists, the issues here are complicated. See Lawrence B. Solum and Max Crema, The Original Meaning of "Due Process of Law" in the Fifth Amendment, *Va. L. Rev.* 108 (2022); Randy Barnett and Evan Bernick, *The Original Meaning of the Fourteenth Amendment* (2021).

6. See John Hart Ely, *Democracy and Distrust* (1981).

reference to tradition. The first category consists of rights guaranteed by the first eight amendments. The Due Process Clause has long been understood to "incorporate" most of those rights (including freedom of speech, press, religion, and assembly) and thus to apply them to the states; the *Dobbs* Court took the relevant cases as given and raised no questions about them.

The second category consists of "a select list of fundamental rights that are not mentioned anywhere in the Constitution."[7] According to the Court, this select list is limited to those that are deeply rooted in tradition and essential to our nation's "scheme of ordered liberty."[8] So understood, the list does not expand or evolve; it does not shift with new values. Recall that the right to marry someone of a different sex would almost certainly qualify as deeply rooted in tradition. So too for the right to have as many children as one would like (within the context of marriage). Noting that "the Constitution makes no mention of abortion,"[9] the Court emphasized that for purposes of evaluating *Roe*, the second category—the "select list of fundamental rights that are not mentioned"—is the relevant one.

But crucially, the Court urged that the analysis of the two categories is *essentially the same*. In the context of incorporation of the Bill of Rights, the Court's decisions have emphasized traditions. In cases involving excessive fines and the right to keep and bear arms—both part of the Bill of Rights—the Court has paid exceedingly close attention to the nation's practices at the time of ratification, and thus the Court has rooted its incorporation holdings in "relevant historical evidence."[10] With respect

7. Dobbs, 142 S.Ct. at 2246.
8. Dobbs, 142 S.Ct. at 2246.
9. Dobbs, 142 S.Ct. at 2240.
10. Dobbs, 142 S.Ct. at 2247.

to incorporation of the Bill of Rights itself, this is a form of due process traditionalism, with a strong originalist theme.[11] In the *Dobbs* Court's view, "it would be anomalous if similar historical support were not required when a putative right is not mentioned anywhere in the Constitution."[12]

This is a key claim, and the *Dobbs* Court was very far from the first to offer it. Similar ideas have occasionally played a role in the Court's rulings.[13] In the *Michael H.* case, allowing states to adopt an irrebuttable presumption that the husband is the father of a child born into his family, Justice Scalia, for a plurality, explicitly embraced due process traditionalism. He argued that careful consideration of specific traditions ensures that judges will remain faithful to "the society's views."[14] This was not originalism; it was a different way of limiting judicial discretion. To decide what the Due Process Clause protects, Justice Scalia wanted to ask whether there is a specific tradition in support of (say) a right to send one's child to a private school, not whether there is an abstract tradition in support of (say) freedom of choice in the large. Justice Scalia urged that the problem with general readings of traditions is that they provide "such imprecise guidance, they permit judges to dictate rather than

11. See Cass R. Sunstein, Due Process Traditionalism, *Mich. L. Rev.* 106 (2008): 1543. On originalist grounds, we might end up being due process traditionalists, because and if the original understanding incorporated tradition. The Dobbs Court does not really argue that this is so, which is why its analysis is best understood as traditionalist *as opposed to* originalist, rather than traditionalist *because* originalist.

12. Dobbs, 142 S.Ct. at 2247.

13. See, e.g., Washington v. Glucksberg, 521 U.S. 702, 720–21 (1997); Michael H. v. Gerald D., 491 U.S. 110, 122–24 (1989); Moore v. City of E. Cleveland, 431 U.S. 494, 503 (1977).

14. Michael H., 491 U.S. at 127n6.

discern the society's views."[15] And if judges are not bound "by any particular, identifiable tradition," they are not bound by the "rule of law at all."[16] Hence, we can see the origins of due process traditionalism in the effort to ensure rule-bound law.

In refusing to recognize a right to assisted suicide in the *Glucksberg* case, the Court also embraced due process traditionalism. The Court emphasized that such a right was not "objectively, deeply rooted in this Nation's history and tradition."[17] There is a direct line from the plurality opinion in *Michael H.* in 1989 to *Glucksberg* in 1997 to *Dobbs* in 2022, and at least some of the incorporation cases support the central idea. Notably, *Glucksberg* seemed, until *Dobbs*, to be a *failed* effort to entrench due process traditionalism, an outlier superseded by *Lawrence*, protecting the right to same-sex sodomy, and *Obergefell,* protecting the right to same-sex marriage. In all of these cases, the Court rejected due process traditionalism. In *Lawrence,* for example, the Court quoted with approval Justice John Paul Stevens's claim: "The fact that the governing majority in a State has traditionally viewed a particular practice as immoral is not a sufficient reason for upholding a law prohibiting the practice; neither history nor tradition could save a law prohibiting miscegenation from constitutional attack."[18] That was then; this is now. *Glucksberg* is back.

According to the *Dobbs* Court, one reason for limiting the term "liberty" by reference to tradition is that the term is "capacious" and there is a "natural human tendency to confuse" what the Fourteenth Amendment "protects with our own ardent

15. Michael H., 491 U.S. at 127n6.
16. Michael H., 491 U.S. at 127n6.
17. Glucksberg, 521 U.S. at 703.
18. Lawrence v. Texas, 539 U.S. 558, 577–78 (2003).

views about the liberty that Americans should enjoy."[19] This is a point about the risks of judicial discretion, especially when judges are tempted to make their own moral readings. With that point in mind, "the Court has long been 'reluctant' to recognize rights that are not mentioned in the Constitution."[20] Unless it respects "the teachings of history," the Court notes, the justices could well fall "into the freewheeling judicial policymaking that characterized discredited decisions such as *Lochner v. New York*."[21] This passage should be taken as a vigorous objection to moral readings of the Constitution; due process traditionalism is invoked as an alternative to a freewheeling Supreme Court. (We can also see it, on this count, as an alternative to Thayerism or originalism.)

Does the right to abortion find support in "relevant historical evidence"? According to the *Dobbs* Court, it does not. Until late in the twentieth century, "there was no support in American law for a constitutional right to obtain an abortion."[22] In every state, "abortion had long been a crime."[23] The common law made abortion "criminal in at least some stages of pregnancy," and in the 1800s, American law "expanded criminal liability for abortions."[24] When the Fourteenth Amendment was adopted, "three-quarters of the States had made abortion a crime at any stage of pregnancy, and the remaining states would soon follow."[25] The *Dobbs* Court offered a great deal of detail in an effort to support these historical claims.

19. Dobbs, 142 S.Ct. at 2247.
20. Dobbs, 142 S.Ct. at 2247.
21. Dobbs, 142 S.Ct. at 2248.
22. Dobbs, 142 S.Ct. at 2248.
23. Dobbs, 142 S.Ct. at 2248.
24. Dobbs, 142 S.Ct. at 2248.
25. Dobbs, 142 S.Ct. at 2248–49.

Consequences

Thus far, then, the *Dobbs* Court's approach to the Due Process Clause seems reasonably straightforward (like it or not). The Due Process Clause does not protect a substantive right unless the purported right can claim support from deeply rooted traditions *and* is essential to ordered liberty as the United States has long understood it. Some rights might claim support from tradition but might not be essential to ordered liberty; consider, as possible examples, the right to eat catfish, the right to be a professional boxer, and the right to cut down trees in one's own backyard. If, by contrast, a state prohibited people from wearing warm clothes in the cold of winter, we might be able to say that it was violating the Due Process Clause as the Court understands it.

For the Court's argument, the largest challenge comes from an assortment of cases purporting to protect "intimate and personal choices" that are "central to personal dignity and autonomy." Some of these are exceedingly hard to square with due process traditionalism.[26] Are they fixed points? Should they be? Consider the following:

- the right to marry a person of a different race (1967)
- the right to live with one's grandchildren (1977)
- the right to use contraceptives within marriage (1965)
- the right to obtain contraceptives within or without marriage (1972)

---

26. If it is applied to the Fifth Amendment as well as the Fourteenth, due process traditionalism is also hard to square with the "equal protection component of the Due Process Clause." For example, Califano v. Goldfarb, 430 U.S. 199 (1977), would be impossible to defend.

- the right to allow one's young children to be educated in a language of one's choice (1923)
- the right to send one's children to private schools (1925)
- the right not to be sterilized without one's consent (1923)
- the right to engage in private, consensual sexual acts among adults (2003)
- the right to marry a person of the same sex (2015)

Are these rights protected by the Due Process Clause? To put it gently: under the method suggested in *Dobbs*, the answer is not clearly yes. To put it less gently: under the method suggested in *Dobbs*, the answer is generally no.

Under due process traditionalism, it would be necessary to ask about the teachings of history *and* about ordered liberty as this nation has understood it. For consensual sexual acts and same-sex marriage, at least, history's teachings do not support a substantive right under the Due Process Clause. With respect to racial intermarriage and living with one's grandchildren, it cannot be said that American history speaks plainly in favor of a constitutional right under the Court's approach. Due process traditionalism fits uneasily with a large number of rulings.

Perhaps with these challenges in mind, the Court did not attempt to show that its prior holdings are, in fact, supportable by reference to an inquiry into traditions and ordered liberty. Instead, the Court urged, the relevant cases did not involve "the critical moral question posed by abortion." The reason is that they did not involve "potential life" or an "unborn human being." This is a gesture in the direction of a more modest opinion, and of course the claim is *true*. But why, exactly, is it *relevant*? The central thrust of the Court's opinion is *not* that the interest in protecting unborn human beings, or the rights of unborn human beings, outweighs, or might reasonably be taken to outweigh, the right to choose. It is that under the framework of due process traditionalism, the right to choose does not fall in the category of interests that are presumed to be protected by the Constitution at all.[27]

The Court was undoubtedly aware that if it really meant to embrace due process traditionalism, it would have to reject a great deal of established law. In any case, the Court accepted, at least for purposes of argument, the proposition that the scope of the Due Process Clause might not be defined by reference to the specific practices of the states at the time that the Fourteenth Amendment was ratified—which would mean that the cases listed above might not have to be ruled. (Again: But on the Court's traditionalist logic, why not?) The *Dobbs* Court emphasized that the right to choose was not protected by our traditions or the idea of ordered liberty. On the contrary, abortion had often been regulated or prohibited in our nation's history. The issue is nothing new; "the fundamental moral question that it poses is ageless"; no "new scientific learning calls for a different answer to the underlying moral question." In this light, the Court concluded, *the only question is the usual one to be asked when a protected right is not at stake: whether restrictions imposed by a legislature are rational.* This is, of course, a critical conclusion; under "rational basis" review, as it is called, legislation is nearly always upheld, because it is very hard to say that it is not

27. Here is a sympathetic understanding of what the Court is doing here: Due process traditionalism is meant to set out the appropriate boundaries of substantive due process. But it is not meant to suggest that every decision that departs from due process traditionalism will be *overruled.* The reference to the uniqueness of the abortion question is meant to suggest why *Roe* and *Casey* should be overruled. Decisions like *Griswold* and *Obergefell* might have been wrong when decided (given due process traditionalism), but they need not and perhaps should not be overruled.

even "rational." The consequence is that if a purported right does not qualify as presumptively protected under the tradition/ordered liberty test, a state is nearly always entitled to act as it chooses. (A little Thayer, anyone?)

To be sure, the state must always have legitimate reasons for imposing restrictions. But under the "rational basis" test as the Court understands it, that is not at all a demanding test. In the context of abortion, those legitimate reasons include "respect for and preservation of prenatal life at all stages of development," as well as "the preservation of the integrity of the medical profession," and "the protection of maternal health and safety."[28] In that light, the Court found it straightforward to uphold the Mississippi law at issue in the case, which prohibited abortions after fifteen weeks of pregnancy.

The Court's opinion thus did three things at once. It (1) offered due process traditionalism as the framework for understanding the protection of substantive rights under the Due Process Clause; (2) sought to preserve, or at least not to reject, existing substantive due process holdings except those involving abortion; and (3) subjected abortion restrictions to rational basis review. The Court aimed to accomplish (2) by emphasizing that abortion involves a unique moral question. That is fair enough. But when we focus on (1), we immediately see that some or many of the existing substantive due process holdings are exceedingly vulnerable. And if we focus on (3), we immediately see that if a purported right is not supported by the tradition/ordered liberty framework of (1), then restrictions on that right will be subject only to rational basis review (and as just noted, such restrictions will almost certainly be upheld).

28. Dobbs, 142 S.Ct. at 2284.

For example, it would not be easy to argue that bans on same-sex marriage are irrational as that term is standardly understood in constitutional law; almost no law is deemed to be "irrational"! Return to the list above. Would *anything* on that list constitute a right, under due process traditionalism, whose infringement would be struck down under rational basis review as it is now understood? Probably not.

It follows that the *Dobbs* Court's efforts to preserve existing substantive due process holdings are unsuccessful. If those holdings survive, it is because they are precedents and to be preserved as such (even though *Roe* was a precedent, and was not preserved as such).

Discretion

As I have suggested, the *Dobbs* Court was intensely concerned with the problem of judicial discretion. The Court did not want courts to seize on the capacious word "liberty" to entrench the justices' own preferred understandings of the concept. For those who share that concern, originalism might seem to be the right solution, and moral readings the worst of all. But the Court's opinion is not really originalist. To be sure, the draft does make a strong gesture toward *textualism*: "Constitutional analysis must begin with 'the language of the instrument,' which offers a 'fixed standard' for ascertaining what our founding document means. The Constitution makes no express reference to a right to obtain an abortion, and therefore those who claim that it protects such a right must show that the right is somehow implicit in the constitutional text."

Still, the Court devoted essentially no attention to the original public meaning of the Due Process Clause, or to the original understanding of its framers and ratifiers. It is possible that due process traditionalism would emerge from the relevant history; but the Court did not defend that conclusion. In this light, the endorsement of due process traditionalism is best seen as a particular form of common-law constitutionalism (with a little Thayerism thrown in for good measure, because "rational basis" review is so deferential to the legislature). That is a compressed claim that requires some explanation.

First: The *Dobbs* opinion can be seen as a form of common-law constitutionalism insofar as it works hard with, and attempts to preserve, existing precedents (with the exception, of course, of those relating to abortion). The Court devoted much more space to prior Supreme Court cases than to the understanding of the Due Process Clause at the time of ratification. In fact, the Court spent no time on the understanding of the Due Process Clause at the time of ratification.

Second: The *Dobbs* opinion is traditionalist insofar as it emphasizes long-standing practices and deplores moral theorizing. It is proudly and self-consciously backward-looking with respect to the definition of liberty. This is its due process traditionalism, and the core of the *Dobbs* ruling.

Third: The opinion is Thayerian insofar as it emphasizes the need to give a wide berth to the judgments of the political process. A constant preoccupation of the opinion is the risk that, unmoored from traditions, judges will be giving liberty the content they like, and so depriving the political process of the authority to make moral judgments.

Regrettably, we need one more ism: Dworkinism. As we saw in chapter 2, Ronald Dworkin argued that in law, interpretation involves "fit" and "justification": judges need to fit the existing legal materials, and within the constraints of fit, they need to put those materials in the best constructive light. The Court worked pretty hard to do that, which means that it might be

approved or criticized on the ground of either fit or justification. The Court urged that its ruling fits its precedents well, or
well enough, and also that its ruling limited the Court's role in
democratic society, which meant that it would be good on
grounds of justification. Despite the Court's efforts to enlist
precedents, *Dobbs* is not exactly wonderful on grounds of fit;
we have seen that due process traditionalism hardly fits all of
the cases. Notably, however, Dworkin also believed that the Supreme Court should be a "forum of principle" in American government. He was no traditionalist. Can a Dworkinian, aiming
to do as well as possible in terms of both fit and justification, be
a traditionalist? Absolutely. The *Dobbs* Court demonstrates the
point. If we think that people of principle would embrace traditionalism, we might embrace *Dobbs*.

Getting Technical

What, exactly, does *Dobbs* do to constitutional law? How does
it jeopardize fixed points? Does it in fact reflect an approach to
constitutional law that we should endorse or admire?

To answer these questions, let us step back a bit. Consider the
following possible understandings of the Due Process Clause of
the Fourteenth Amendment (the list is not exhaustive):

1. The Clause is purely procedural. It guarantees fair
   process, period. It protects no substantive rights at all.
2. The Clause is largely procedural. It guarantees fair
   process. But it also has a substantive dimension insofar
   as it includes substantive protection of the rights laid out
   in the first eight amendments. Otherwise it is not
   substantive at all.

3. The Clause is largely procedural, but it includes substantive protection of the first eight amendments. It also includes substantive protection of unenumerated rights that were widely understood as fundamental at the time of ratification, and that were taken to be fundamental in the particular sense that they were essential to ordered liberty. This is, of course, the understanding of the Court in *Dobbs*.

4. The Clause is substantive as well as procedural, and for purposes of both substance and procedure, the concept of "liberty" *is not frozen in time*. It develops in common-law fashion. The development is principled, but it is not backward-looking, or at least it is not *exclusively* backward-looking. The development singles out actions or interests that are central to people's autonomy and their self-conception. That is the understanding of the Court in many modern due process cases, including *Roe*, *Lawrence*, and *Obergefell*.

With respect to the Court in *Dobbs* and *Roe*, the contest is between (3) and (4). To be sure, one could embrace (4) while also thinking that *Roe* was wrong (if, for example, one thought that the interest in protecting unborn life was strong enough to override the woman's right).

How shall we choose among the four alternatives? Department of the Obvious: To answer that question, we need a theory of interpretation. If we are originalists, the choice among competing views is largely historical. What was the original public meaning of the Due Process Clause? To say the least, the answer to that question is disputed, and it gets pretty technical in a hurry. The topic is complicated by the Privileges or

Immunities Clause. Recall the relevant text of the Fourteenth Amendment:

> No State shall make or enforce any law which shall abridge the privileges or immunities of citizens of the United States; nor shall any State deprive any person of life, liberty, or property, without due process of law.

What is the relationship between the Due Process Clause and the Privileges or Immunities Clause? We might favor a purely procedural reading of the Due Process Clause, in the form of (1) or (2) above, and insist that the Fourteenth Amendment's substantive clause is the Privileges or Immunities Clause. If so, we would be open to the possibility that the Privileges or Immunities Clause protects a host of substantive rights. If so, we would need to identify the privileges or immunities. What are they? On that question, we might again have a contest between a view that would be close to (3) and one that would be close to (4).[29] That is, we might take the Privileges or Immunities Clause to protect rights that are recognized by tradition or take the same clause to license judges to engage in moral readings, recognizing rights that are in some sense new. In *Dobbs*, the Court recognized the question by way of a footnote, where it is urged that even if the Privileges or Immunities Clause is the proper source of substantive rights, those rights "would need to be rooted in the Nation's history and tradition."[30] Hence (3).

---

29. I emphasize the word "might"; I am not attempting here to offer a view on interpretation of the Privileges or Immunities Clause, originalist or otherwise, and therefore not insisting that the right interpretation is (3) or (4). On one view, for example, the category of privileges or immunities is very large, but anything within the category is subject to reasonable regulation.

30. There are also questions about the Ninth Amendment. On a reasonable view, that amendment applies to the national government (whatever it means), and if it

We Are the Ancients

Dobbs makes a strong stand in favor of (3); for decades the Court mostly opted for (4). How should the contest between (3) and (4) be resolved?

Originalists would look to history. But imagine that we are not originalists and that we think that the choice must be defended not by reference to history but as a matter of principle. Suppose that we believed, with reason, that long-standing traditions are excellent, or excellent enough, and that judicial judgments, with respect to the content of "liberty," are highly unreliable. Suppose too that we believed that democratic thinking about that concept will broaden the idea of liberty over time, when it deserves to be broadened. If so, we should endorse (3) and reject (4); we have no need for (4).

Or suppose we believed, with reason, that long-standing traditions are not excellent, or not excellent enough, in the sense that they will not include certain practices within the domain of "liberty" that deserve to be included. Suppose too that we believed that judicial judgments, with respect to the content of liberty, are likely to be reliable. Suppose finally that we believed that democratic processes will sometimes fail to protect liberty when it ought to be protected. If so, we would favor (4) and reject (3).

In insisting on "the forum of principle," Dworkin himself favored (4) on roughly that ground. There are no proofs here, but in my view the arc of American history tends to support his view. Note that the choice between (3) and (4) depends on a

---

applies to the states, it would be because it is incorporated via the Fourteenth Amendment, most plausibly through the Privileges or Immunities Clause. (As they say: Awkward.) It is broadly consistent with the overall approach of the Court to say that if the Ninth Amendment does anything of relevance (a big if), it adds nothing to the Fourteenth Amendment, even if it is incorporated.

long-standing contest between Burkeans, who emphasize the importance of respecting long-standing traditions, and non-Burkeans, who turn longevity against them. Those who reject Burke urge in response that *we are the ancients*. They believe in progress on multiple fronts. Consider the words of Blaise Pascal, the French mathematician and philosopher:

> Those whom we call ancient were really new in all things, and properly constituted the infancy of mankind; and as we have joined to their knowledge the experience of the centuries which have followed them, it is in ourselves that we should find this antiquity that we revere in others. They should be admired for the results which they derived from the very few principles they possessed, and they should be excused for those in which they failed rather from the lack of the advantage of experience than the strength of reasoning.[31]

The British philosopher Jeremy Bentham spoke in similar terms, urging that "the wisdom of times called old" is in reality "the wisdom of the cradle."[32] One version of this idea is that we know much more about facts. We create vaccines. We produce cell phones and electric cars. We build airplanes and laptops. Another version of this idea is that there is *moral* progress. We have learned a few things about liberty and equality. Consider, for example, what we have learned about democracy and who is entitled to participate in it; about freedom of speech; about equality on the basis of race; about equality on the basis of sex.

It is true that even if we believe that (and we should), we need not think that Supreme Court justices, consisting of a small

31. Blaise Pascal, *Thoughts, Letters and Minor Works*, trans. O. W. Wight, ed. Charles W. Eliot (1910), 449.
32. Jeremy Bentham, *Fallacies of Authority* (1824), 71.

group of not-young lawyers, should be authorized to understand the Constitution to incorporate their own assessments of what they think we have learned, or of what they have learned. But Supreme Court justices live in society, and perhaps we might agree that some forms of moral progress are legitimately introduced, by them, into judgments about basic rights. (I believe that.) At the very least, a commitment to (4), and a rejection of (3), must depend on a belief of that general sort.

Consider, then, an alternative to due process traditionalism, also with foundations in existing law: The Due Process Clause gives substantive protection to a certain category of interests, which qualify as rights because they are so fundamental to people's autonomy and self-determination. The right not to buckle one's seatbelt does not fall within that category. The right to use contraceptives does, and so does the right to live with one's grandchildren. The list of rights that fall within the protected category is to be developed cautiously, but it is not frozen and closed. It depends on the relevant arguments and on questions of principle. On this view, *Roe* might be right, though one can embrace this view without *necessarily* thinking that *Roe* was right; that question turns on the legitimacy and importance of protecting unborn life, a question on which reasonable people can disagree.

What the Constitution Mentions

This statement by the *Dobbs* Court is true: "[T]he Constitution makes no mention of abortion."[33] It is also true that the Constitution makes no mention of the following:

- education
- segregation

33. Dobbs, 142 S.Ct. at 2240.

- sterilization
- blasphemy
- libel
- false statements of fact
- incitement
- sedition
- obscenity
- commercial advertising
- expenditures on political campaigns
- school prayer
- one person, one vote
- the right to vote[34]
- sex discrimination[35]
- affirmative action
- injury in fact
- regulations that diminish the value of property

This is a list of just a few of the things that the Constitution does not mention that have been taken to give rise to serious constitutional challenges, and in many cases to invalidation of state or federal legislation. Should we say that because the Constitution does not mention education, *Brown v. Board of Education* was wrong? In the 1950s, many critics of *Brown* said exactly that. Shall we say that because the Constitution does not mention defamation or libel, *New York Times v. Sullivan* was wrong? Shall we say that because the Constitution does not mention affirmative action, the Court has been wrong to strike down affirmative action programs? These are preposterous questions. The Constitution speaks of "freedom of speech"; it does not

---

34. The Fifteenth and Twenty-Fourth Amendments are exceptions.
35. With the exception of the Nineteenth Amendment.

speak of criticism of the president, or libel, or blasphemy, or use of vulgar language. The Constitution speaks of "the equal protection of the laws"; it does not speak of juries, police, fire, or education. We need to know what the general language means. What *Dobbs* is saying is that at least when we are dealing with the Due Process Clause of the Fourteenth Amendment, courts should cabin their analysis by asking about the content of tradition.

That suggestion raises a fundamental question: How are we to assess rulings that protect the right to sexual privacy and to same-sex marriage—rights that are emphatically nontraditionalist (and also non-Thayerian)? Should we be constitutional traditionalists in general? Free speech traditionalists in particular? Property rights traditionalists? Equal protection traditionalists?

It is natural to answer that *Dobbs* was only about the Due Process Clause of the Fourteenth Amendment. Perhaps the Court's insistence on traditionalism is limited to that Clause. If so, *Dobbs* has nothing at all to say about the rest of the Constitution, including Article I, Article III, the First Amendment, the Second Amendment, the Fifth Amendment, or the Equal Protection Clause. Perhaps that is correct. Perhaps the Court should be taken to be embracing due process traditionalism without committing itself to any other kind of traditionalism. But as we have seen, the traditionalism in *Dobbs* cannot be simply "read off" the Due Process Clause. It is meant as a way of making best sense of the Clause, and of the Court's own precedents. (Recall that it seems to be incorporated by reference into the Court's understanding of the Privileges or Immunities Clause.) If the Court likes due process traditionalism, perhaps it will embrace traditionalism in other areas as well. And indeed, the Court has shown growing interest in constitutional traditionalism quite broadly. Is that a good idea? Would it make sense to incorporate traditionalism into the Supreme Court's thinking about freedom of speech? Should the scope of the freedom of speech be defined by reference to traditions? Should traditions be defined as they stood as of 1789? As of 1868?

We should notice that while "the freedom of speech" is a narrower concept than "liberty," it is not exactly narrow, and it can be specified in many different ways. We should also notice that, just as with the Fourteenth Amendment, there is a "natural human tendency to confuse" what the First Amendment "protects with our own ardent views about the [freedom of speech] that Americans should enjoy." Ought judges to be keenly interested in the reach of the concept of the freedom of speech before ratification of the First Amendment, or before ratification of the Fourteenth Amendment, perhaps for originalist reasons, or perhaps for traditionalist reasons?

Or consider the reach of the Equal Protection Clause. The words "school segregation" do not appear in the Fourteenth Amendment; the words "sex discrimination" do not appear there, either. Ought we to be nervous about judicial deployment about a broad concept like equality, for fear that there is a "natural human tendency to confuse" what the Fourteenth Amendment "protects with our own ardent views about the [equality] that Americans should enjoy"? These questions could easily proliferate.

Let us suppose that the theoretical foundations of the *Dobbs* opinion would *not* be applied to many constitutional questions that do not involve the Due Process Clause. Let us suppose that traditionalism makes sense for that clause but not for other clauses. If so, it must be because that particular clause is best understood to protect (only) those substantive rights that are vindicated by tradition, whereas (for example) the First Amendment is best understood to establish broad principles whose reach encompasses rights that extend well beyond those vindicated by tradition, and (for example) the Equal Protection Clause is best understood to establish broad principles of non-discrimination that extend well beyond what tradition establishes.[36] If we think that the First Amendment and the Equal Protection Clause are best understood in this way, it must be because we are comfortable, or comfortable enough, with the moral judgments, informed but not defined by tradition, that judges are inevitably required to make.

If we are comfortable, or comfortable enough, with those judgments, it must be because we are not, and should not be, across-the-board traditionalists. It must be because we are at best ambivalent traditionalists (on principle; recall Pascal and Bentham). It must be because we believe in some forms of moral progress, and have at least some faith in the judicial capacity to incorporate one or more of those forms of progress in constitutional law.

To be a bit more detailed and a bit more explicit: To say the least, abortion is a hard issue, and reasonable people reach different conclusions about it, including reasonable people who think about constitutional law. My topic in this chapter has been traditionalism, not abortion. We could imagine a world in which traditionalism would make sense—a world in which traditions were good or good enough, or excellent, and in which judges, thinking about moral questions, would blunder badly. In my view, that world is not our world. With respect to traditions,

36. On that issue, see Cass R. Sunstein, Sexual Orientation and the Constitution: A Note on the Relationship between Due Process and Equal Protection, *U. Chi. L. Rev.* 55 (1988): 1161.

our history is excellent in many ways, but not so excellent in others. Cautious judges, making moral judgments about what liberty entails, can do better than traditions; consider the protection of sexual privacy in general, or the protection of same-sex marriage. To the extent that we can trust our judges, moral readings, understanding liberty in ways that go beyond tradition, would lead to a better system of constitutional law.

Traditionalism is not a self-evidently bad foundation for constitutional rights. But in our world, it is not good enough.

6

Where to Stand

OUR LITTLE tale is now complete. There are many plausible theories of interpretation. Nothing in the Constitution itself requires any of them or rules any of them off the table.[1] Though we might wish it otherwise, the choice is our own. The oath of office is very important, but it requires fidelity to the Constitution, not to any particular theory of how to interpret it.

To choose a theory of interpretation, we need to try to seek reflective equilibrium, which means that fixed points are highly relevant, even if they are merely provisional. You might think that a theory of interpretation that allows certain kinds of atrocities and barbarism is unlikely to be an acceptable theory of interpretation. Your view of what counts as an atrocity or a barbarism might be different from those of other people. You might think it exceedingly important that a theory of interpretation produces a lot of stability or sharply confines the discretion of judges. Other people might not find that to be particularly important or even desirable.

---

1. Textualism is a possible exception; but for reasons stated in the text, even that is complicated.

Disagreements about how to interpret the Constitution seem to be about many things, but they are really about only one thing: Differences in the reflective equilibrium that different people are able to approach or attain. To be sure, none of us has entirely worked it out; all of us are uncertain about some important things. But in deciding how to interpret the Constitution, we have to think about what we are most firmly committed to, and about what we are least likely to be willing to give up. Without thoughts of that sort, we are at sea; we lack moorings. We cannot know what to think and why to think it. We might be inclined to believe that judges should follow the original public meaning of the Constitution, but when asked why we think that, we have to give some answers, and once we do that, things will get complicated, and we will rapidly be thinking about how to reach reflective equilibrium. The same is true if we are inclined to say that judges should be Thayerians or should give moral readings of the Constitution. Saying one of those things might seem appealing, but it, too, raises a host of questions, and the search for reflective equilibrium is on.

That is why people disagree about how to interpret the Constitution. For some people, the stability and predictability associated with originalism are strong positives. For others, they are mostly illusory, and not positives at all. For some people, a theory of interpretation that allows judges to make moral judgments is out of bounds for that very reason. For other people, such a theory has considerable appeal.

For some people, a theory of interpretation that allows states to segregate people by race is essentially disqualified for that reason. For (a few) others, a conclusion to that effect is a point of pride. For still others, it is essentially neither here nor there, because what they want, from a theory of interpretation, are abstract and general goods (perhaps the rule of law, perhaps protection against judicial tyranny), not results in particular cases. Disagreements on these points capture a large part of what people are disagreeing about, when they disagree about the right theory of constitutional interpretation.

No theory makes sense for every imaginable world. On certain assumptions about courts, legislatures, and presidents—on certain assumptions about who is good at what—something like Thayerism would be an excellent idea. If judges were systematically confused or malevolent, we should be inclined to embrace Thayerism. On other assumptions, some forms of originalism would be attractive as well. If originalism led to a system of institutions and rights that we should enthusiastically embrace, then we might well want to embrace originalism enthusiastically. To be sure, a lot of work would have to be done to specify the right form of originalism and to show that it would lead to that admirable system.

The strongest objection to originalism is that it would not, in fact, do that. That objection is convincing (in my view). But rejection of originalism, like rejection of Thayerism, depends on some judgments and some projections about likely futures—which suggests, yet again, that the choice of a theory of interpretation depends on judgments about what is most likely to unfold under different theories of interpretation. We could imagine a world in which originalism is best, just as we could imagine a world in which Thayerism is best. I do not believe that either world is our world, but I might be wrong. We could, for example, imagine a future of horrible moral readings by judges whose morality is abhorrent, in which case we might hope ardently for originalism or Thayerism.

Traditionalism would be appealing if traditions were excellent. Whether we love traditions or despise them, there is no a priori argument against constitutional traditionalism. In an imaginable world, it is a terrific idea. In the abstract, we might be tempted to think it is a terrific idea in our own world. But if we look carefully at our complex traditions (which include slavery and segregation), at the long arc of constitutional law, and at the many rights that have emerged from careful scrutiny of traditions, we are unlikely to be so excited about traditionalism. There are no proofs here, but there is progress over time, including moral progress, and that progress deserves to be reflected in constitutional law.

Those, then, are my central claims. But by way of conclusion, shall we expand the viewscreen? Shall we be blunt? Shall we be a little reckless? Consider the following propositions:

1. The Constitution does not forbid maximum hour and minimum wage laws.
2. *Brown v. Board of Education* was correctly decided; the Constitution does not permit racial segregation.
3. The Supreme Court has been right to strike down laws that discriminate on the basis of sex.
4. The First Amendment should be understood to give very broad protection to political speech, subject to the qualification in (5).
5. The Supreme Court should be much less aggressive in reviewing restrictions on campaign contributions and campaign expenditures.
6. The Supreme Court should be much less aggressive than it has been in reviewing restrictions on commercial advertising.
7. The Supreme Court was wrong to hold that "political gerrymandering" presents a political question, not subject to judicial review.
8. The Constitution allows Congress to grant broad discretion to administrative agencies.

9. *Griswold v. Connecticut*, protecting the right of married couples to use contraceptives, was correctly decided.

10. The Supreme Court should continue to allow the existence of independent agencies, such as the Federal Communications Commission and the Federal Trade Commission.

In my view, all of these propositions are correct. Indeed, they are *clearly* correct. Out of the closet we come: These are my fixed points; they are part of my reflective equilibrium, such as it is.

Propositions (1), (2), and (3) are inconsistent with originalism and Thayerism. Proposition (7) is consistent with originalism, but that is not why I believe it to be true; the same can be said of propositions (4) and (5). Propositions (6), (9), and (10) may or may not be consistent with originalism. Nonetheless, I believe them to be true.

Now consider these propositions:

1. The Court was right to recognize a right to same-sex marriage.

2. *Roe v. Wade* badly overreached; the Court should have decided the case more narrowly.

3. *Dobbs* was wrongly decided; the Court should not have overruled *Roe v. Wade*.

4. The Court was correct to recognize an individual right to gun ownership in *Heller v. District of Columbia*, but some of its subsequent decisions have read that right too broadly.

5. The Supreme Court should allow educational institutions a lot of room to create race-conscious affirmative action programs, designed to benefit Black Americans.

In my view, all of these propositions are also correct, but none of them is *clearly* correct. Reasonable people can differ. But I do believe that they are correct. None of them is correct because originalism is correct, though there is an argument that (14) and (15) are correct on originalist grounds. Propositions (11) and (14) are inconsistent with Thayerism.

My views about propositions (1) through (15), and my greater conviction about some propositions than others, are based on judgments about the appropriate arc of constitutional law, with an understanding of the development of governing principles over time. Two general ideas, both traceable to the founding itself, play a large role in that understanding. Both of them can be seen as fixed points (and good ones).

The first is the idea of *deliberative democracy*, mentioned in chapter 1. Philosophers, political scientists, historians, and academic lawyers have elaborated this idea both as a matter of principle and as a reading of the American constitutional tradition.[2] The central idea is that well-functioning systems of self-government place a high premium on accountability. We the People are sovereign, and that admittedly abstract idea has a host of implications for voting and self-government, and for the judicial role in protecting them. But deliberative democracies also place a high premium on reflection and reason-giving. Such systems are democratic in the sense that the voters have

---

2. See Joseph Bessette, *The Mild Voice of Reason* (1994); Jürgen Habermas, *Between Facts and Norms* (1985); Jon Elster, ed., *Deliberative Democracy* (1991); Amy Gutmann and Dennis Thompson, *Democracy and Disagreement* (1998); Andrae Beachtiger et al., eds., *The Oxford Handbook of Deliberative Democracy* (2008); Michael Neblo, *Deliberative Democracy between Theory and Practice* (2015).

ultimate control (not over everything, but over a lot). They are deliberative in the sense that majority rule is not enough. Outcomes must also be justified by reasons. "Because we say so" is never a sufficient justification for the imposition of burdens or the denial of benefits. If, for example, a political majority discriminates against the elderly, or imposes large costs on some group, it must explain itself. "Naked preferences" are forbidden.

The idea of deliberative democracy plays a large role in my support for propositions (1), (4), (5), (6), (7), (8), and (10). The authors of the Constitution believed in deliberative democracy, and the U.S. Constitution is best understood as an effort to create one. True, we cannot claim, and should not claim, that the specific propositions I support here can be defended by reference to originalism. Still, constitutional law should be developed with close reference to the idea of deliberative democracy.[3]

The second idea is an *anticaste principle*, which forbids the creation of second-class citizenship, and which informs existing constitutional law with respect to equality, particularly in the domain of discrimination on the basis of race, sex, and sexual orientation.[4] The idea is traceable to the republican commitments of the founding era, though it was patently violated until the Civil War Amendments (and is, in various ways, violated today). As Justice Harlan wrote in *Plessy v. Ferguson*, "There is no caste here."[5]

3. Long ago I tried to defend that view. See Cass R. Sunstein, *The Partial Constitution* (1993).

4. See Cass R. Sunstein, The Anticaste Principle, *Mich. L. Rev.* 92 (1994): 2410.

5. Plessy v. Ferguson, 163 U.S. 537, 559 (1896) (Harlan, J., dissenting).

The anticaste principle plays a large role in my support for propositions (2), (3), and (15) above. The authors of the Thirteenth, Fourteenth, and Fifteenth Amendments believed in an anticaste principle, and their handiwork can be understood as an effort to entrench that principle. The republicanism of the founding period was rooted in a commitment to political equality, which can be taken to embed a kind of anticaste principle. True, we cannot claim, and should not claim, that the specific propositions I support here can be defended by reference to originalism. Still, constitutional law should be developed with close reference to the anticaste principle.

I am acutely aware that development of the idea of deliberative democracy, and of the anticaste principle, would take a great deal of work. I aim only to point in their direction here, and to signal their centrality to the particular approach to constitutional law that I favor.[6]

In its most extreme forms, Thayerism is close to an algorithm: uphold everything. But Thayer himself did not embrace extreme Thayerism (good for him!). In some hands, originalism purports to be an algorithm, but it is hardly that. And if it were an algorithm, we should not follow it.

We post a sign: No Algorithms Here. As we live it, constitutional law is not a matter of deduction. It is rooted in a common-law process, one of case-by-case decision making, in which identifiable moral aspirations and commitments play a central role, and in which defining constitutional rulings are animated

6. One last time: These views are contingent on some judgments about the likely performance of institutions and those who populate them. If judges are stupid or evil, Thayerism looks a lot better. And if the democratic process is highly reliable, we might think Thayerism is just right, or we might at most be drawn to democracy-reinforcing understandings of judicial review of the sort explained and embraced by Ely.

by an insistence on deliberative democracy and the anticaste principle. We could do a lot worse; we cannot do a lot better.

———

Recall these words from James Jackson, a representative from Georgia, in 1789: "Our Constitution is like a vessel just launched, and lying at the wharf, she is untried, and you can hardly discover any one of her properties."[7] About 150 years after Jackson spoke, Franklin Delano Roosevelt said that "we revere" the founding document "not because it is old but because it is ever new, not in the worship of its past alone but in the faith of the living who keep it young, now and in the years to come."

The vessel is no longer lying at the wharf. She is tried. You can discover her properties. They are a product of the faith of the living who keep her young.

7. See Jonathan Gienapp, *The Second Creation* (2018), 1.

ACKNOWLEDGMENTS

Thanks go first to two wonderful colleagues and teachers: Stephen Breyer and Adrian Vermeule. I was privileged to teach a seminar with Breyer in the fall of 2022 and with Vermeule in the spring of 2022; the two seminars gave shape to this book. Thanks too to the students in both seminars, whose extraordinary comments and suggestions much improved the arguments here.

My editor, Bridget Flannery-McCoy, fundamentally reoriented the plan of the book. She also provided several rounds of detailed comments on the manuscript, which made everything much better. I am very grateful to her.

Participants in workshops at the University of Chicago Law School, the University of Liverpool Law School, and Harvard Law School were a great help. For exceptionally valuable comments on all or part of the manuscript, I thank Benjamin Eidelson, Stephen Sachs, and Vermeule. Special thanks to Conor Casey and Larry Solum for superb comments on early drafts that made this book much better. I am also grateful to three anonymous readers for many helpful suggestions. Thanks also to Dean John Manning for many discussions, and to him, and Harvard Law School, for support over the summer of 2022, when much of this book was written. Zachary Goldstein provided extraordinary research assistance.

While almost all the material in this book is new, chapter 2 draws on "There Is Nothing That Interpretation Just Is," *Constitutional Commentary* 30 (2015). I am grateful to the editors for permission to do that here.

INDEX

A NOTE ON THE TYPE

This book has been composed in Arno, an Old-style serif typeface in the classic Venetian tradition, designed by Robert Slimbach at Adobe.

THE CONSTITUTION
OF THE UNITED STATES

We the People of the United States, in Order to form a more perfect Union, establish Justice, insure domestic Tranquility, provide for the common defence, promote the general Welfare, and secure the Blessings of Liberty to ourselves and our Posterity, do ordain and establish this Constitution for the United States of America.

Article I

Section 1: Congress

All legislative Powers herein granted shall be vested in a Congress of the United States, which shall consist of a Senate and House of Representatives.

Section 2: The House of Representatives

The House of Representatives shall be composed of Members chosen every second Year by the People of the several States, and the Electors in each State shall have the Qualifications requisite for Electors of the most numerous Branch of the State Legislature.

No Person shall be a Representative who shall not have attained to the Age of twenty five Years, and been seven Years a Citizen of the United States, and who shall not, when elected, be an Inhabitant of that State in which he shall be chosen.

Representatives and direct Taxes shall be apportioned among the several States which may be included within this Union, according to their respective Numbers, which shall be determined by adding to the whole Number of free Persons, including those bound to Service for a Term of Years, and excluding Indians not taxed, three fifths of all other Persons. The actual Enumeration shall be made within three Years after the first Meeting of the Congress of the United States, and within every subsequent Term of ten Years, in such Manner as they shall by Law direct. The number of Representatives shall not exceed one for every thirty Thousand, but each State shall have at Least one Representative; and until such enumeration shall be made, the

State of New Hampshire shall be entitled to chuse three, Massachusetts eight, Rhode-Island and Providence Plantations one, Connecticut five, New-York six, New Jersey four, Pennsylvania eight, Delaware one, Maryland six, Virginia ten, North Carolina five, South Carolina five, and Georgia three.

When vacancies happen in the Representation from any State, the Executive Authority thereof shall issue Writs of Election to fill such Vacancies.

The House of Representatives shall chuse their Speaker and other Officers; and shall have the sole Power of Impeachment.

Section 3: *The Senate*

The Senate of the United States shall be composed of two Senators from each State, chosen by the Legislature thereof, for six Years; and each Senator shall have one Vote.

Immediately after they shall be assembled in Consequence of the first Election, they shall be divided as equally as may be into three Classes. The Seats of the Senators of the first Class shall be vacated at the Expiration of the second Year, of the second Class at the Expiration of the fourth Year, and of the third Class at the Expiration of the sixth Year, so that one third may be chosen every second Year; and if Vacancies happen by Resignation, or otherwise, during the Recess of the Legislature of any State, the Executive thereof may make temporary Appointments until the next Meeting of the Legislature, which shall then fill such Vacancies.

No Person shall be a Senator who shall not have attained to the Age of thirty Years, and been nine Years a Citizen of the United States, and who shall not, when elected, be an Inhabitant of that State for which he shall be chosen.

The Vice President of the United States shall be President of the Senate, but shall have no Vote, unless they be equally divided.

The Senate shall chuse their other Officers, and also a President pro tempore, in the Absence of the Vice President, or when he shall exercise the Office of President of the United States.

The Senate shall have the sole Power to try all Impeachments. When sitting for that Purpose, they shall be on Oath or Affirmation. When the President of the United States is tried, the Chief Justice shall preside: And no Person shall be convicted without the Concurrence of two thirds of the Members present.

Judgment in Cases of Impeachment shall not extend further than to removal from Office, and disqualification to hold and enjoy any Office of honor, Trust or Profit under the United States: but the Party convicted shall nevertheless be liable and subject to Indictment, Trial, Judgment and Punishment, according to Law.

Section 4: Elections

The Times, Places and Manner of holding Elections for Senators and Representatives, shall be prescribed in each State by the Legislature thereof; but the Congress may at any time by Law make or alter such Regulations, except as to the Places of chusing Senators.

The Congress shall assemble at least once in every Year, and such Meeting shall be on the first Monday in December, unless they shall by Law appoint a different Day.

Section 5: Powers and Duties of Congress

Each House shall be the Judge of the Elections, Returns and Qualifications of its own Members, and a Majority of each shall constitute a Quorum to do Business; but a smaller Number may adjourn from day to day, and may be authorized to compel the Attendance of absent Members, in such Manner, and under such Penalties as each House may provide.

Each House may determine the Rules of its Proceedings, punish its Members for disorderly Behaviour, and, with the Concurrence of two thirds, expel a Member.

Each House shall keep a Journal of its Proceedings, and from time to time publish the same, excepting such Parts as may in their Judgment require Secrecy; and the Yeas and Nays of the Members of either House on any question shall, at the Desire of one fifth of those Present, be entered on the Journal.

Neither House, during the Session of Congress, shall, without the Consent of the other, adjourn for more than three days, nor to any other Place than that in which the two Houses shall be sitting.

Section 6: Rights and Disabilities of Members

The Senators and Representatives shall receive a Compensation for their Services, to be ascertained by Law, and paid out of the Treasury of the United States. They shall in all Cases, except Treason, Felony and Breach of the Peace, be privileged from Arrest during their Attendance at the Session of their respective Houses, and in going to and returning from the same; and for any Speech or Debate in either House, they shall not be questioned in any other Place.

No Senator or Representative shall, during the Time for which he was elected, be appointed to any civil Office under the Authority of the United States, which shall have been created, or the Emoluments whereof shall have been increased during such time; and no Person holding any Office under the United States, shall be a Member of either House during his Continuance in Office.

Section 7: Legislative Process

All Bills for raising Revenue shall originate in the House of Representatives; but the Senate may propose or concur with Amendments as on other Bills.

Every Bill which shall have passed the House of Representatives and the Senate, shall, before it become a Law, be presented to the President of the United States; If he approve he shall sign it, but if not he shall return it, with his Objections to that House in which it shall have originated, who shall enter the Objections at large on their Journal, and proceed to reconsider it. If after such Reconsideration two thirds of that House shall agree to pass the Bill, it shall be sent, together with the Objections, to the other House, by which it shall likewise be reconsidered, and if approved by two thirds of that House, it shall become a Law. But in all such Cases the Votes of both Houses shall be determined by Yeas and Nays, and the Names of the Persons voting for and against the Bill shall be entered on the Journal of each House respectively. If any Bill shall not be returned by the President within ten Days (Sundays excepted) after it shall have been presented to him, the Same shall be a Law, in like Manner as if he had signed it, unless the Congress by their Adjournment prevent its Return, in which Case it shall not be a Law.

Every Order, Resolution, or Vote to which the Concurrence of the Senate and House of Representatives may be necessary (except on a question of Adjournment) shall be presented to the President of the United States; and before the Same shall take Effect, shall be approved by him, or being disapproved by him, shall be repassed by two thirds of the Senate and House of Representatives, according to the Rules and Limitations prescribed in the Case of a Bill.

Section 8: Powers of Congress

The Congress shall have Power To lay and collect Taxes, Duties, Imposts and Excises, to pay the Debts and provide for the common Defence and general Welfare of the United States; but all Duties, Imposts and Excises shall be uniform throughout the United States;

To borrow Money on the credit of the United States;

To regulate Commerce with foreign Nations, and among the several States, and with the Indian Tribes;

To establish a uniform Rule of Naturalization, and uniform Laws on the subject of Bankruptcies throughout the United States;

To coin Money, regulate the Value thereof, and of foreign Coin, and fix the Standard of Weights and Measures;

To provide for the Punishment of counterfeiting the Securities and current Coin of the United States;

To establish Post Offices and post Roads;

To promote the Progress of Science and useful Arts, by securing for limited Times to Authors and Inventors the exclusive Right to their respective Writings and Discoveries;

To constitute Tribunals inferior to the supreme Court;

To define and punish Piracies and Felonies committed on the high Seas, and Offenses against the Law of Nations;

To declare War, grant Letters of Marque and Reprisal, and make Rules concerning Captures on Land and Water;

To raise and support Armies, but no Appropriation of Money to that Use shall be for a longer Term than two Years;

To provide and maintain a Navy;

To make Rules for the Government and Regulation of the land and naval Forces;

To provide for calling forth the Militia to execute the Laws of the Union, suppress Insurrections and repel Invasions;

To provide for organizing, arming, and disciplining, the Militia, and for governing such Part of them as may be employed in the Service of the United States, reserving to the States respectively, the Appointment of the Officers, and the Authority of training the Militia according to the discipline prescribed by Congress;

To exercise exclusive Legislation in all Cases whatsoever, over such District (not exceeding ten Miles square) as may, by Cession of particular States, and the Acceptance of Congress, become the Seat of the Government of the United States, and to exercise like Authority over all Places purchased by the Consent of the Legislature of the State in which the Same shall be, for the Erection of Forts, Magazines, Arsenals, dock-Yards and other needful Buildings;-And

To make all Laws which shall be necessary and proper for carrying into Execution the foregoing Powers, and all other Powers vested by this Constitution in the Government of the United States, or in any Department or Officer thereof.

Section 9: Powers Denied Congress

The Migration or Importation of such Persons as any of the States now existing shall think proper to admit, shall not be prohibited by the Congress prior to the Year one thousand eight hundred and eight, but a Tax or duty may be imposed on such Importation, not exceeding ten dollars for each Person.

The Privilege of the Writ of Habeas Corpus shall not be suspended, unless when in Cases of Rebellion or Invasion the public Safety may require it.

No Bill of Attainder or ex post facto Law shall be passed.

No Capitation, or other direct, Tax shall be laid, unless in Proportion to the Census or Enumeration herein before directed to be taken.

No Tax or Duty shall be laid on Articles exported from any State.

No Preference shall be given by any Regulation of Commerce or Revenue to the Ports of one State over those of another: nor shall Vessels bound to, or from, one State, be obliged to enter, clear, or pay Duties in another.

No Money shall be drawn from the Treasury, but in Consequence of Appropriations made by Law; and a regular Statement and Account of the Receipts and Expenditures of all public Money shall be published from time to time.

No Title of Nobility shall be granted by the United States: And no Person holding any Office of Profit or Trust under them, shall, without the Consent of the Congress, accept of any present, Emolument, Office, or Title, of any kind whatever, from any King, Prince, or foreign State.

Section 10: Powers Denied to the States

No State shall enter into any Treaty, Alliance, or Confederation; grant Letters of Marque and Reprisal; coin Money; emit Bills of Credit; make any Thing but gold and silver Coin a Tender in Payment of Debts; pass any Bill of Attainder, ex post facto Law, or Law impairing the Obligation of Contracts, or grant any Title of Nobility.

No State shall, without the Consent of the Congress, lay any Imposts or Duties on Imports or Exports, except what may be absolutely necessary for executing it's inspection Laws: and the net Produce of all Duties and Imposts, laid by any State on Imports or Exports, shall be for the Use of the Treasury of the United States; and all such Laws shall be subject to the Revision and Control of the Congress.

No State shall, without the Consent of Congress, lay any Duty of Tonnage, keep Troops, or Ships of War in time of Peace, enter into any Agreement or Compact with another State, or with a foreign Power, or engage in War, unless actually invaded, or in such imminent Danger as will not admit of delay.

Article II

Section 1

The executive Power shall be vested in a President of the United States of America.

He shall hold his Office during the Term of four Years, and, together with the Vice President, chosen for the same Term, be elected, as follows:

Each State shall appoint, in such Manner as the Legislature thereof may direct, a Number of Electors, equal to the whole Number of Senators and Representatives to which the State may be entitled in the Congress: but no Senator or Representative, or Person holding an Office of Trust or Profit under the United States, shall be appointed an Elector.

The Electors shall meet in their respective States, and vote by Ballot for two Persons, of whom one at least shall not be an Inhabitant of the same State with themselves. And they shall make a List of all the Persons voted for, and of the Number of Votes for each; which List they shall sign and certify, and transmit sealed to the Seat of the Government of the United States, directed to the President of the Senate. The President of the Senate shall, in the Presence of the Senate and House of Representatives, open all the Certificates, and the Votes shall then be counted. The Person having the greatest Number of Votes shall be the President, if such Number be a Majority of the whole Number of Electors appointed; and if there be more than one who have such Majority, and have an equal Number of Votes, then the House of Representatives shall immediately chuse by Ballot one of them for President; and if no Person have a Majority, then from the five highest on the List the said House shall in like Manner chuse the President. But in chusing the President, the Votes shall be taken by States, the Representation from each State having one Vote; A quorum for this Purpose shall consist of a Member or Members from two thirds of the States, and a Majority of all the States shall be necessary to a Choice. In every Case, after the Choice of the President, the Person having the greatest Number of Votes of the Electors shall be the Vice President. But if there should remain two or more who have equal Votes, the Senate shall chuse from them by Ballot the Vice President.

The Congress may determine the Time of chusing the Electors, and the Day on which they shall give their Votes; which Day shall be the same throughout the United States.

No Person except a natural born Citizen, or a Citizen of the United States, at the time of the Adoption of this Constitution, shall be eligible to the Office of President; neither shall any person be eligible to that Office who shall not have attained to the Age of thirty five Years, and been fourteen Years a Resident within the United States.

In Case of the Removal of the President from Office, or of his Death, Resignation, or Inability to discharge the Powers and Duties of the said Office, the Same shall devolve on the Vice President, and the Congress may by Law provide for the Case of Removal, Death, Resignation or Inability, both of the President and Vice President, declaring what Officer shall then act as President, and such Officer shall act accordingly, until the Disability be removed, or a President shall be elected.

The President shall, at stated Times, receive for his Services, a Compensation, which shall neither be increased nor diminished during the Period for which he shall have been elected, and he shall not receive within that Period any other Emolument from the United States, or any of them.

Before he enter on the Execution of his Office, he shall take the following Oath or Affirmation:—"I do solemnly swear (or affirm) that I will faithfully execute the

Office of President of the United States, and will to the best of my Ability, preserve, protect and defend the Constitution of the United States."

Section 2

The President shall be Commander in Chief of the Army and Navy of the United States, and of the Militia of the several States, when called into the actual Service of the United States; he may require the Opinion, in writing, of the principal Officer in each of the executive Departments, upon any Subject relating to the Duties of their respective Offices, and he shall have Power to grant Reprieves and Pardons for Offenses against the United States, except in Cases of Impeachment.

He shall have Power, by and with the Advice and Consent of the Senate, to make Treaties, provided two thirds of the Senators present concur; and he shall nominate, and by and with the Advice and Consent of the Senate, shall appoint Ambassadors, other public Ministers and Consuls, Judges of the supreme Court, and all other Officers of the United States, whose Appointments are not herein otherwise provided for, and which shall be established by Law: but the Congress may by Law vest the Appointment of such inferior Officers, as they think proper, in the President alone, in the Courts of Law, or in the Heads of Departments.

The President shall have Power to fill up all Vacancies that may happen during the Recess of the Senate, by granting Commissions which shall expire at the End of their next Session.

Section 3

He shall from time to time give to the Congress Information of the State of the Union, and recommend to their Consideration such Measures as he shall judge necessary and expedient; he may, on extraordinary Occasions, convene both Houses, or either of them, and in Case of Disagreement between them, with Respect to the Time of Adjournment, he may adjourn them to such Time as he shall think proper; he shall receive Ambassadors and other public Ministers; he shall take Care that the Laws be faithfully executed, and shall Commission all the Officers of the United States.

Section 4

The President, Vice President and all civil Officers of the United States, shall be removed from Office on Impeachment for, and Conviction of, Treason, Bribery, or other high Crimes and Misdemeanors.

Article III

Section 1

The judicial Power of the United States, shall be vested in one supreme Court, and in such inferior Courts as the Congress may from time to time ordain and establish. The Judges, both of the supreme and inferior Courts, shall hold their Offices during good Behaviour, and shall, at stated Times, receive for their Services, a Compensation, which shall not be diminished during their Continuance in Office.

Section 2

The judicial Power shall extend to all Cases, in Law and Equity, arising under this Constitution, the Laws of the United States, and Treaties made, or which shall be made, under their Authority;—to all Cases affecting Ambassadors, other public Ministers and Consuls;—to all Cases of admiralty and maritime Jurisdiction;—to Controversies to which the United States shall be a Party;—to Controversies between two or more States;—between a State and Citizens of another State;—between Citizens of different States;—between Citizens of the same State claiming Lands under Grants of different States, and between a State, or the Citizens thereof, and foreign States, Citizens or Subjects.

In all Cases affecting Ambassadors, other public Ministers and Consuls, and those in which a State shall be Party, the supreme Court shall have original Jurisdiction. In all the other Cases before mentioned, the supreme Court shall have appellate Jurisdiction, both as to Law and Fact, with such Exceptions, and under such Regulations as the Congress shall make.

The Trial of all Crimes, except in Cases of Impeachment; shall be by Jury; and such Trial shall be held in the State where the said Crimes shall have been committed; but when not committed within any State, the Trial shall be at such Place or Places as the Congress may by Law have directed.

Section 3

Treason against the United States, shall consist only in levying War against them, or in adhering to their Enemies, giving them Aid and Comfort. No Person shall be convicted of Treason unless on the Testimony of two Witnesses to the same overt Act, or on Confession in open Court.

The Congress shall have Power to declare the Punishment of Treason, but no Attainder of Treason shall work Corruption of Blood, or Forfeiture except during the Life of the Person attainted.

Article IV

Section 1

Full Faith and Credit shall be given in each State to the public Acts, Records, and judicial Proceedings of every other State. And the Congress may by general Laws prescribe the Manner in which such Acts, Records and Proceedings shall be proved, and the Effect thereof.

Section 2

The Citizens of each State shall be entitled to all Privileges and Immunities of Citizens in the several States.

A Person charged in any State with Treason, Felony, or other Crime, who shall flee from Justice, and be found in another State, shall on Demand of the executive Authority of the State from which he fled, be delivered up, to be removed to the State having Jurisdiction of the Crime.

No Person held to Service or Labour in one State, under the Laws thereof, escaping into another, shall, in Consequence of any Law or Regulation therein, be discharged from such Service or Labour, but shall be delivered up on Claim of the Party to whom such Service or Labour may be due.

Section 3

New States may be admitted by the Congress into this Union; but no new State shall be formed or erected within the Jurisdiction of any other State; nor any State be formed by the Junction of two or more States, or Parts of States, without the Consent of the Legislatures of the States concerned as well as of the Congress.

The Congress shall have Power to dispose of and make all needful Rules and Regulations respecting the Territory or other Property belonging to the United States; and nothing in this Constitution shall be so construed as to Prejudice any Claims of the United States, or of any particular State.

Section 4

The United States shall guarantee to every State in this Union a Republican Form of Government, and shall protect each of them against Invasion; and on Application of the Legislature, or of the Executive (when the Legislature cannot be convened) against domestic Violence.

Article V

The Congress, whenever two thirds of both Houses shall deem it necessary, shall propose Amendments to this Constitution, or, on the Application of the Legislatures of two thirds of the several States, shall call a Convention for proposing Amendments, which, in either Case, shall be valid to all Intents and Purposes, as Part of this Constitution, when ratified by the Legislatures of three fourths of the several States, or by Conventions in three fourths thereof, as the one or the other Mode of Ratification may be proposed by the Congress; Provided that no Amendment which may be made prior to the Year One thousand eight hundred and eight shall in any Manner affect the first and fourth Clauses in the Ninth Section of the first Article; and that no State, without its Consent, shall be deprived of its equal Suffrage in the Senate.

Article VI

All Debts contracted and Engagements entered into, before the Adoption of this Constitution, shall be as valid against the United States under this Constitution, as under the Confederation.

This Constitution, and the Laws of the United States which shall be made in Pursuance thereof; and all Treaties made, or which shall be made, under the Authority of the United States, shall be the supreme Law of the Land; and the Judges in every State shall be bound thereby, any Thing in the Constitution or Laws of any State to the Contrary notwithstanding.

The Senators and Representatives before mentioned, and the Members of the several State Legislatures, and all executive and judicial Officers, both of the United States and of the several States, shall be bound by Oath or Affirmation, to support this Constitution; but no religious Test shall ever be required as a Qualification to any Office or public Trust under the United States.

Article VII

The Ratification of the Conventions of nine States, shall be sufficient for the Establishment of this Constitution between the States so ratifying the Same.

First Amendment

Congress shall make no law respecting an establishment of religion, or prohibiting the free exercise thereof; or abridging the freedom of speech, or of the press; or the right of the people peaceably to assemble, and to petition the Government for a redress of grievances.

Second Amendment

A well regulated Militia, being necessary to the security of a free State, the right of the people to keep and bear Arms, shall not be infringed.

Third Amendment

No Soldier shall, in time of peace be quartered in any house, without the consent of the Owner, nor in time of war, but in a manner to be prescribed by law.

Fourth Amendment

The right of the people to be secure in their persons, houses, papers, and effects, against unreasonable searches and seizures, shall not be violated, and no Warrants shall issue, but upon probable cause, supported by Oath or affirmation, and particularly describing the place to be searched, and the persons or things to be seized.

Fifth Amendment

No person shall be held to answer for a capital, or otherwise infamous crime, unless on a presentment or indictment of a Grand Jury, except in cases arising in the land or naval forces, or in the Militia, when in actual service in time of War or public danger; nor shall any person be subject for the same offence to be twice put in jeopardy of life or limb; nor shall be compelled in any criminal case to be a witness against himself, nor be deprived of life, liberty, or property, without due process of law; nor shall private property be taken for public use, without just compensation.

Sixth Amendment

In all criminal prosecutions, the accused shall enjoy the right to a speedy and public trial, by an impartial jury of the State and district wherein the crime shall have been committed, which district shall have been previously ascertained by law, and to be informed of the nature and cause of the accusation; to be confronted with the witnesses against him; to have compulsory process for obtaining witnesses in his favor, and to have the Assistance of Counsel for his defence.

Seventh Amendment

In Suits at common law, where the value in controversy shall exceed twenty dollars, the right of trial by jury shall be preserved, and no fact tried by a jury, shall be otherwise reexamined in any Court of the United States, than according to the rules of the common law.

Eighth Amendment

Excessive bail shall not be required, nor excessive fines imposed, nor cruel and unusual punishments inflicted.

Ninth Amendment

The enumeration in the Constitution, of certain rights, shall not be construed to deny or disparage others retained by the people.

10th Amendment

The powers not delegated to the United States by the Constitution, nor prohibited by it to the States, are reserved to the States respectively, or to the people.

11th Amendment

The Judicial power of the United States shall not be construed to extend to any suit in law or equity, commenced or prosecuted against one of the United States by Citizens of another State, or by Citizens or Subjects of any Foreign State.

12th Amendment

The Electors shall meet in their respective states and vote by ballot for President and Vice-President, one of whom, at least, shall not be an inhabitant of the same state with themselves; they shall name in their ballots the person voted for as President, and in distinct ballots the person voted for as Vice-President, and they shall make distinct lists of all persons voted for as President, and of all persons voted for as Vice-President, and of the number of votes for each, which lists they shall sign and certify, and transmit sealed to the seat of the government of the United States, directed to the President of the Senate;—The President of the Senate shall, in the presence of the Senate and House of Representatives, open all the certificates and the votes shall then be counted;—The person having the greatest number of votes for President, shall be the President, if such number be a majority of the whole number of Electors appointed; and if no person have such majority, then from the persons having the highest numbers not exceeding three on the list of those voted for as President, the House of Representatives shall choose immediately, by ballot, the President. But in choosing the President, the votes shall be taken by states, the representation from each state having one vote; a quorum for this purpose shall consist of a member or members from two-thirds of the states, and a majority of all the states shall be necessary to a choice. And if the House of Representatives shall not choose a President whenever the right of choice shall devolve upon them, before the fourth day of March next following, then the Vice-President shall act as President, as in case of the death or other constitutional disability of the President.—The person having the greatest number of votes as Vice-President, shall be the Vice-President, if such number be a majority of the whole number of Electors appointed, and if no person have a majority, then from the two highest numbers on the list, the Senate shall choose the Vice-President; a quorum for the purpose shall consist of two-thirds of the whole number of Senators, and a majority of the whole number shall be necessary to a choice. But no person constitutionally ineligible to the office of President shall be eligible to that of Vice-President of the United States.

13th Amendment

Section 1

Neither slavery nor involuntary servitude, except as a punishment for crime whereof the party shall have been duly convicted, shall exist within the United States, or any place subject to their jurisdiction.

Section 2

Congress shall have power to enforce this article by appropriate legislation.

14th Amendment

Section 1

All persons born or naturalized in the United States, and subject to the jurisdiction thereof, are citizens of the United States and of the State wherein they reside. No State shall make or enforce any law which shall abridge the privileges or immunities of citizens of the United States; nor shall any State deprive any person of life, liberty, or property, without due process of law; nor deny to any person within its jurisdiction the equal protection of the laws.

Section 2

Representatives shall be apportioned among the several States according to their respective numbers, counting the whole number of persons in each State, excluding Indians not taxed. But when the right to vote at any election for the choice of electors for President and Vice-President of the United States, Representatives in

Congress, the Executive and Judicial officers of a State, or the members of the Legislature thereof, is denied to any of the male inhabitants of such State, being twenty-one years of age, and citizens of the United States, or in any way abridged, except for participation in rebellion, or other crime, the basis of representation therein shall be reduced in the proportion which the number of such male citizens shall bear to the whole number of male citizens twenty-one years of age in such State.

Section 3

No person shall be a Senator or Representative in Congress, or elector of President and Vice-President, or hold any office, civil or military, under the United States, or under any State, who, having previously taken an oath, as a member of Congress, or as an officer of the United States, or as a member of any State legislature, or as an executive or judicial officer of any State, to support the Constitution of the United States, shall have engaged in insurrection or rebellion against the same, or given aid or comfort to the enemies thereof. But Congress may by a vote of two-thirds of each House, remove such disability.

Section 4

The validity of the public debt of the United States, authorized by law, including debts incurred for payment of pensions and bounties for services in suppressing insurrection or rebellion, shall not be questioned. But neither the United States nor any State shall assume or pay any debt or obligation incurred in aid of insurrection or rebellion against the United States, or any claim for the loss or emancipation of any slave; but all such debts, obligations and claims shall be held illegal and void.

Section 5

The Congress shall have the power to enforce, by appropriate legislation, the provisions of this article.

15th Amendment
Section 1

The right of citizens of the United States to vote shall not be denied or abridged by the United States or by any State on account of race, color, or previous condition of servitude.

Section 2

The Congress shall have the power to enforce this article by appropriate legislation.

16th Amendment

The Congress shall have power to lay and collect taxes on incomes, from whatever source derived, without apportionment among the several States, and without regard to any census or enumeration.

17th Amendment

The Senate of the United States shall be composed of two Senators from each State, elected by the people thereof, for six years; and each Senator shall have one vote. The electors in each State shall have the qualifications requisite for electors of the most numerous branch of the State legislatures.

When vacancies happen in the representation of any State in the Senate, the executive authority of such State shall issue writs of election to fill such vacancies: Provided, That the legislature of any State may empower the executive thereof to make temporary appointments until the people fill the vacancies by election as the legislature may direct.

This amendment shall not be so construed as to affect the election or term of any Senator chosen before it becomes valid as part of the Constitution.

18th Amendment

Section 1

After one year from the ratification of this article the manufacture, sale, or transportation of intoxicating liquors within, the importation thereof into, or the exportation thereof from the United States and all territory subject to the jurisdiction thereof for beverage purposes is hereby prohibited.

Section 2

The Congress and the several States shall have concurrent power to enforce this article by appropriate legislation.

Section 3

This article shall be inoperative unless it shall have been ratified as an amendment to the Constitution by the legislatures of the several States, as provided in the Constitution, within seven years from the date of the submission hereof to the States by the Congress.

19th Amendment

The right of citizens of the United States to vote shall not be denied or abridged by the United States or by any State on account of sex.

Congress shall have power to enforce this article by appropriate legislation.

20th Amendment

Section 1

The terms of the President and the Vice President shall end at noon on the 20th day of January, and the terms of Senators and Representatives at noon on the 3d day of January, of the years in which such terms would have ended if this article had not been ratified; and the terms of their successors shall then begin.

Section 2

The Congress shall assemble at least once in every year, and such meeting shall begin at noon on the 3d day of January, unless they shall by law appoint a different day.

Section 3

If, at the time fixed for the beginning of the term of the President, the President elect shall have died, the Vice President elect shall become President. If a President shall not have been chosen before the time fixed for the beginning of his term, or if the President elect shall have failed to qualify, then the Vice President elect shall act as President until a President shall have qualified; and the Congress may by law provide for the case wherein neither a President elect nor a Vice President shall have qualified, declaring who shall then act as President, or the manner in which one who is to act shall be selected, and such person shall act accordingly until a President or Vice President shall have qualified.

Section 4

The Congress may by law provide for the case of the death of any of the persons from whom the House of Representatives may choose a President whenever the right of choice shall have devolved upon them, and for the case of the death of any of the persons from whom the Senate may choose a Vice President whenever the right of choice shall have devolved upon them.

Section 5

Sections 1 and 2 shall take effect on the 15th day of October following the ratification of this article.

Section 6

This article shall be inoperative unless it shall have been ratified as an amendment to the Constitution by the legislatures of three-fourths of the several States within seven years from the date of its submission.

21st Amendment

Section 1

The eighteenth article of amendment to the Constitution of the United States is hereby repealed.

Section 2

The transportation or importation into any State, Territory, or Possession of the United States for delivery or use therein of intoxicating liquors, in violation of the laws thereof, is hereby prohibited.

Section 3

This article shall be inoperative unless it shall have been ratified as an amendment to the Constitution by conventions in the several States, as provided in the Constitution, within seven years from the date of the submission hereof to the States by the Congress.

22nd Amendment

Section 1

No person shall be elected to the office of the President more than twice, and no person who has held the office of President, or acted as President, for more than two years of a term to which some other person was elected President shall be elected to the office of President more than once. But this Article shall not apply to any person holding the office of President when this Article was proposed by Congress, and shall not prevent any person who may be holding the office of President, or acting as President, during the term within which this Article becomes operative from holding the office of President or acting as President during the remainder of such term.

Section 2

This article shall be inoperative unless it shall have been ratified as an amendment to the Constitution by the legislatures of three-fourths of the several States within seven years from the date of its submission to the States by the Congress.

23rd Amendment

Section 1

The District constituting the seat of Government of the United States shall appoint in such manner as Congress may direct:

A number of electors of President and Vice President equal to the whole number of Senators and Representatives in Congress to which the District would be entitled if it were a State, but in no event more than the least populous State; they shall be in addition to those appointed by the States, but they shall be considered, for the purposes of the election of President and Vice President, to be electors appointed by a State; and they shall meet in the District and perform such duties as provided by the twelfth article of amendment.

Section 2

The Congress shall have power to enforce this article by appropriate legislation.

24th Amendment

Section 1

The right of citizens of the United States to vote in any primary or other election for President or Vice President, for electors for President or Vice President, or for Senator or Representative in Congress, shall not be denied or abridged by the United States or any State by reason of failure to pay poll tax or other tax.

Section 2

The Congress shall have power to enforce this article by appropriate legislation.

25th Amendment

Section 1

In case of the removal of the President from office or of his death or resignation, the Vice President shall become President.

Section 2

Whenever there is a vacancy in the office of the Vice President, the President shall nominate a Vice President who shall take office upon confirmation by a majority vote of both Houses of Congress.

Section 3

Whenever the President transmits to the President pro tempore of the Senate and the Speaker of the House of Representatives his written declaration that he is unable to discharge the powers and duties of his office, and until he transmits to them a written declaration to the contrary, such powers and duties shall be discharged by the Vice President as Acting President.

Section 4

Whenever the Vice President and a majority of either the principal officers of the executive departments or of such other body as Congress may by law provide, transmit to the President pro tempore of the Senate and the Speaker of the House of Representatives their written declaration that the President is unable to discharge the powers and duties of his office, the Vice President shall immediately assume the powers and duties of the office as Acting President.

Thereafter, when the President transmits to the President pro tempore of the Senate and the Speaker of the House of Representatives his written declaration that no inability exists, he shall resume the powers and duties of his office unless the Vice President and a majority of either the principal officers of the executive department or of such other body as Congress may by law provide, transmit within four days to the President pro tempore of the Senate and the Speaker of the House of Representatives their written declaration that the President is unable to discharge the powers and duties of his office. Thereupon Congress shall decide the issue, assembling within forty-eight hours for that purpose if not in session. If the Congress, within twenty-one days after receipt of the latter written declaration, or, if Congress is not in session, within twenty-one days after Congress is required to assemble, determines by two-thirds vote of both Houses that the President is unable to discharge the powers and duties of his office, the Vice President shall continue to discharge the same as Acting President; otherwise, the President shall resume the powers and duties of his office.

26th Amendment

Section 1

The right of citizens of the United States, who are eighteen years of age or older, to vote shall not be denied or abridged by the United States or by any State on account of age.

Section 2

The Congress shall have power to enforce this article by appropriate legislation.

27th Amendment

No law, varying the compensation for the services of the Senators and Representatives, shall take effect, until an election of representatives shall have intervened.